Jubal Anderson Early

# Jackson's Campaign against Pope, in August, 1862

An Address by Lieut. Gen'l Jubal A. Early before the First Annual Meeting

of the Association of the Maryland Line

Jubal Anderson Early

**Jackson's Campaign against Pope, in August, 1862**
*An Address by Lieut. Gen'l Jubal A. Early before the First Annual Meeting of the Association of the Maryland Line*

ISBN/EAN: 9783337064747

Printed in Europe, USA, Canada, Australia, Japan

Cover: Foto ©ninafisch / pixelio.de

More available books at **www.hansebooks.com**

# JACKSON'S CAMPAIGN AGAINST POPE

IN AUGUST, 1862.

AN

# ADDRESS

-BY-

## Lieut. Gen'l JUBAL A. EARLY

BEFORE THE

## FIRST ANNUAL MEETING

OF THE

## Association of the Maryland Line,

TOGETHER WITH THE

## PROCEEDINGS AT THE THIRD ANNUAL BANQUET

OF THE

## SOCIETY OF THE ARMY AND NAVY OF THE CONFEDERATE STATES,

IN THE STATE OF MARYLAND.

# First Annual Meeting of the Association of the Maryland Line, at the Academy of Music, Baltimore, February 22, 1883.

The meeting was called to order by Maj. Gen'l I. R. Trimble, the senior Governor of the Association, who introduced General Bradley T. Johnson, the President, who he said would bring to their attention matters of deep interest to all Marylanders and to which he invoked their serious consideration.

General Johnson said:

Ladies and Gentlemen: We welcome you with pleasure to this first annual meeting of the Association of the Maryland Line, and we thank you for the cordial greeting you have given us. We have organized ourselves for the purpose of collecting materials for the history of the battles and the bivouacs, the marches and the campaigns of Maryland men in the Confederate Army, and of trying to make some provision for our infirm, disabled and broken comrades, disabled by wounds or broken by the hardships of fortune and of time. We have succeeded greatly in the first object of our endeavors, for we have collected copies of the muster rolls of every Regiment, Battalion and Battery, and are engaged in gathering those of Maryland companies which served in South Carolina and Virginia regiments. Our record is approaching completion.

The pious labor of caring for our comrades still presses us. As the march lengthens, more and more of them fall out of ranks. We have neither pensions or bounties to hope for, nor to rely on. Maryland has given ten millions in bounties to soldiers who enlisted in Maryland regiments on the Union side, and the Union has bestowed two hundred millions in pensions for its defenders. We can only look to ourselves, and to that kind-hearted sympathy and love, which in Maryland has never failed the unfortunate. We hope in time to found a home in which old and infirm Confederate soldiers may be tenderly and respectfully sheltered, and that their old age and honorable scars may be spared at least the public poorhouse. We ask alms from no one; we beg no obolus for Belisarius. We do desire the aid of sympathizing hearts and generous hands. We will continue our efforts with faith in our success. After this brief explanation of the objects of our organization, I perform a duty incumbent on me, which is alike a pleasure and an honor, of introducing to you a soldier whose genius and courage have won for him an illustrious place in the annals of the art of war, and his devotion, sincerity and patriotism the innermost one in the hearts of his countrymen. I introduce to you Lieut. Gen. Jubal A. Early, late commander of the second corps of the Army of Northern Virginia.

Mr. President and Gentlemen of the Maryland Line; my friends and comrades of the Army and Navy of the Confederate States: *Ladies and Gentlemen :—*

When I consented to deliver an address before this Association, and selected the subject of that address, I had no thought that the campaign of August, 1862, in Northern Virginia, would, in any way, be involved in any question or discussion that might arise in Congress, during its present session. It was, therefore, with no reference whatever to the questions which have arisen before that body that I selected my subject. I have long thought the campaign I refer to was not fully appreciated, even by many Confederate officers who participated in it; and I know that some have entertained very erroneous views and made very inaccurate statements in regard to it.

It was my fortune to bear a more active part in that campaign, from its beginning to its close, than any officer, now surviving, who was engaged in it on our side; and I think I know more in respect to its operations, especially those conducted by him whose command bore the most conspicuous part, than any man now living. Hence it was that I selected that campaign as the subject of my address; and I bespeak your indulgence while I attempt to describe it to you. As a matter of necessity, I shall be compelled to omit, or notice very briefly, many interesting events, by reason of the limited time and space which I feel warranted in devoting to the subject on this occasion.

## Campaign against Pope in August, 1862.

The operations of the Army of Northern Virginia, under General Lee, at the close of June and beginning of July, 1862, against the forces under McClellan, generally known as the "Seven days' Battles," had resulted in relieving Richmond of the siege threatening that City, and forced McClellan to take refuge at his "new base" on James River, where it was impracticable to attack him except at great disadvantage. The Army then returned to the vicinity of Richmond, for the purpose of repose after its arduous and harrassing struggle, and to be convenient to the needed supplies.

A new commander, Major general John Pope, had now appeared in Northern Virginia, East of the Blue Ridge and North of the Rapidan, at the head of an army styled the "Army of Virginia," and composed of the corps of McDowell, Banks, and Fremont— the latter then commanded by Sigel.

General Pope, on assuming his new command, had gone to it on a train decked with banners and flying streamers, and had issued a bombastic and vain-glorious address to his troops, in which he said: "I have come to you from the West, where we have always seen the backs of our enemies—from an army whose business it has been to seek the adversary and beat him when found—whose policy has been attack, not defence. * * * I presume I have been called here to pursue the same system, and to lead you against the enemy."

He said further to his troops: "I desire you to dismiss from your minds certain phrases which I am sorry to find much in vogue among you. I hear constantly of taking strong positions and holding them—of lines of retreat and bases of supplies. Let us discard such ideas.- The strongest position which a soldier should desire to occupy is the one from which he can most easily advance upon the enemy. Let us study the probable lines of retreat of our opponents, and leave our own to take care of themselves. Let us look before and not behind. Success and glory are in the advance. Disaster and shame lurk in the rear."

He also proclaimed that his "head-quarters would be in the saddle."

He subsequently issued an order, in which he directed that his troops should subsist upon the country in which their operations were carried on; and two others of a more barbarous character, whose atrocities it is needless to specify. He was certainly producing a great commotion in the poultry yards of the worthy matrons of that region, whose husbands or sons were absent in the service of their state and country, when General Lee sent Stonewall Jackson to look after this redoubtable warrior.

General Jackson's command, at that time, consisted of his own division of four brigades, Lawton's, Winder's, Taliaferro's, and

J. R. Jones's.* Ewell's division of three brigades, Trimble's, Hays's, and my own, and twelve batteries of artillery of about four guns each.

Ewell's division, which was in the advance, reached Gordonsville about the middle of July. Jackson's division soon followed, and General Jackson himself arrived on the 19th. Robertson's brigade of cavalry, of four regiments, and Captain Elijah White's independent company of cavalry, reached the vicinity about the time of Ewell's arrival.

About the last of July, General A. P. Hill's division arrived, it having been ordered to re-inforce General Jackson. In the meantime, there had been several small skirmishes and fights with portions of the enemy's cavalry, which crossed the Rapidan on reconnoitring expeditions and advanced to Orange C. H., and on one or two occasions towards Gordonsville; but of these it is not necessary to speak more particularly.

On the 30th of July, General Halleck, who had been appointed General in chief of the U. S. Army, with his residence at Washington, telegraphed McClellan: "A dispatch just received from General Pope says that deserters report that the enemy is moving south of James River, and that the force in Richmond is very small. I suggest he be pressed in that direction, so as to ascertain the facts of the case."

On the 31st, he again telegraphed McClellan: "General Pope again telegraphs that the enemy is reported to be evacuating Richmond and falling back on Danville and Lynchburg."

On the 1st of August, General Jackson's whole command, exclusive of the cavalry, but including the artillery, could not have exceeded 20,000 officers and men, for duty.

I have in my possession, now, the original monthly returns of the brigades of Ewell's division for the month of July, and the office copy of the consolidated returns for the division, all dated the 31st of the month, and these show present for duty on that day, in the infantry and artillery of the division, 4,801 officers and men, including among the officers all general and staff officers, and even

*NOTE.—This brigade is called "Campbell's brigade" in General Jackson's report, from the fact that it had been commanded by Colonel Campbell during the Valley Campaign of 1862; but General J. R. Jones had been assigned to it, and was in command of it during a portion of the seven days battles. He was now absent sick. In some of the reports it is called the "2nd brigade."

the surgeons and chaplains. I have also the original return of Lawton's brigade for the 13th of August, when it was transferred to Ewell's division, and that shows present for duty in the infantry and artillery of the brigade, 2,099 officers and men. This brigade had not been engaged in the battle of Cedar Run, and the return fully covers its strength on the 1st of the month. The other three brigades of Jackson's division were very small, and 3,000 would probably cover their whole strength. The whole command, therefore, did not exceed 9,900, exclusive of the cavalry, before the arrival of Hill's division. That division, as shown by the returns given by Colonel Walter H. Taylor, in his "Four years with General Lee," had, on the 20th of July, the date of the last return given before the campaign against Pope, for duty, 519 officers and 10,104 enlisted men—in all 10,623. Jackson's whole command, therefore, after Hill's arrival, exclusive of the cavalry, could not have much exceeded 20,000 officers and men for duty, and its effective force, which embraces only enlisted men for duty, was considerably less. The cavalry could not have reached 1,500.

Pope, in his testimony before the Committee on the conduct of the war, on the 8th of July, 1862, said: "I have a movable force, aside from the few troops that are here around Washington and in the intrenchments, of about 43,000 men."

He further said: "I have no apprehension, with my troops stationed in that position, [that is, off on the flanks of any opposing force,] although I have but 43,000 men, that even 80,000 of the enemy would be able to get to Washington at all."

In his official report, dated January 27th, 1863, speaking of the strength of his three corps at the time he was assigned to the command, (June 26th,) he says, "Their effective strength of infantry and artillery, as reported to me, was as follows: Fremont's corps, eleven thousand five hundred strong; Banks's corps reported at fourteen thousand five hundred but in reality only about eight thousand; McDowell's corps eighteen thousand four hundred, making a total of thirty-eight thousand men. The cavalry numbered about five thousand, but most of it was badly mounted and armed, and in poor condition for service."

Thus he estimates his available effective strength at 43,000 men, by deducting 6,400 from Banks's official return-count that and there would be 49,400. It must be borne in mind that the effective strength of an army, embraces only the enlisted men for duty who bear arms.

The statement of Pope, that most of his cavalry "was badly mounted and armed, and in poor condition for service," is calculated to elicit a smile from the survivors of our cavalry, when they recollect that they had to furnish their own horses, and that nearly all their arms were captured from the enemy.

On the 6th of August, Halleck telegraphed McClellan: "You will immediately send a regiment of cavalry and several batteries of artillery to Burnside's command at Aquia Creek. It is reported that Jackson is moving North with a very large force."

Pope was now calling lustily for re-inforcements, and they were getting badly scared at Washington.

## Battle of Cedar Run or Slaughter's Mountain.

Having been informed that a portion of Pope's force was at Culpeper C. H., on the 6th of August, General Jackson determined to advance against it, with the hope of defeating it before re-inforcements could arrive, and orders were given for that purpose. At this time Ewell's division was encamped near Liberty Mills, on the road to Madison C. H., Hill's at Orange C. H., and Jackson's in the vicinity of Gordonsville, while the cavalry watched the crossings of the Rapidan. Ewell's division moved first and crossed the Rapidan, at Liberty Mills, early on the morning of the 7th, being preceded by the 6th Virginia cavalry, under Colonel T. S. Flournoy, and White's company. The cavalry moved out in the direction of Madison C. H., while Ewell turned to the right and moved to the vicinity of Barnett's Ford, where a road to Culpeper C. H. crosses the Rapidan, and bivouacked for the night. The other divisions were to cross at this ford on the 8th and follow Ewell's. Early on the morning of the 8th Ewell's division moved past Barnett's Ford, and drove a cavalry picket from it. Robertson then crossed at that ford with three of his regiments, and, passing to the front, encountered a considerable force of the enemy's cavalry, which he drove across Robertson River, on the road to Culpeper C. H., pursuing it some three or four miles beyond that river. Ewell's division crossed Robertson River early in the day, and bivouacked on its north bank, to await the arrival of the other divisions to within supporting distance. Jackson's division crossed at Barnett's Ford late in the day, but no part of Hill's crossed until the morning of the 9th.

On the morning of that day, Ewell's division moved to the front with my brigade in advance, until we reached the point to which Robertson had advanced with his cavalry, and we found it about eight or nine miles from Culpeper C. H., confronted by a considerable force of the enemy's cavalry in some fields between the Culpeper road and Slaughter's Mountain on the right.

Between the Culpeper road and and the base of the mountain, there is a valley, on a branch of Cedar Run, in which are the large fields of several adjacent farms, the valley as well as the mountain being entirely on the East or right of the road. The country on the West or left of the road, at this point, is mostly wooded, and the road crosses one or two small streams or rivulets running from the West, leaving narrow strips of woodland on the side next the valley, which is otherwise cleared of timber to and beyond the northern end of the mountain; on the northern slope of which is the farm and dwelling of the Rev. Mr. Slaughter. Cedar Run flows beyond, in a south-easterly direction, past the base of the northern end of the mountain.

After a reconnoissance of the enemy's cavalry, some pieces of artillery opened fire on it, causing it to retire; but some of the enemy's pieces, which were concealed from our view, soon responded, and the cavalry returned to its former position.

My brigade was now moved out on the Culpeper road, to its intersection with a road from Madison C. H. about a mile from the point at which we found Robertson. It was here concealed from the view of the enemy by the woods, and his cavalry was concealed from my view by an intervening ridge in the field where it was posted. Trimble's brigade was moved to the right into a body of pines near the base of the mountain, Hays's brigade, under Colonel Forno, being in the rear, near a house at which we found Robertson.

About one o'clock, in the afternoon, I received an order from General Jackson, through a staff officer, to advance with my brigade on the road to Culpeper C. H., with the information that General Ewell would advance, on the right, over the northern slope of the mountain, with his other two brigades, and that I would be followed and supported by General Winder with three brigades of Jackson's division, Lawton's being in the rear guarding the trains; but I was directed not to begin the movement until Winder was in reach and ready to follow me.

While waiting to hear from Winder, General Robertson and myself rode out into the fields on my right, to ascertain the exact position of the enemy's cavalry. The road, a short distance in my front, crossed a small stream running from the left, and then passed through a large body of woods, leaving a long narrow strip on the side next the enemy's cavalry. I could not therefore move along the road by flank in safety, and determined to move obliquely across the road upon the enemy, and then through the fields in line.

On my return to my command, I found a messenger from Winder, with the information that he was ready.

The brigade, which had been diminished on the advance, in the morning, by a regiment and six companies of another detached to picket some side roads, was then moved into a meadow on the stream in my front, on the right of the road, and from that point advanced against the enemy, with the 13th Virginia, under Colonel James A. Walker, deployed as skirmishers to cover my left flank. Colonel Walker was ordered to advance to the front through the woods, clear the road, and gradually oblique to the right, so as to rejoin the brigade on its left, as it moved to the front through the fields. The left of Colonel Walker's skirmish line encountered about a squadron of cavalry, on moving forward, which was driven off by a fire from that flank, and when the brigade reached the crest of the ridge, behind which the main body of the cavalry was posted, the latter was found mounted with the vedettes drawn in, the alarm of approaching danger having been given by the firing on Walker's left. A few shots from the brigade, and from the right of Walker's skirmishers, sent the enemy scampering to the rear. The brigade then wheeled to the left and moved forward through the fields, until it came to a farm road leading from Mrs. Crittenden's house, on the right, to and across the Culpeper road.

At the point where the farm road crossed the Culpeper road, the latter emerged from the woods, and, running for about three hundred yards, with a prolongation of the main body of woods on the left and a field on its right, passed between a wheatfield on the left and a cornfield on the right, and then crossed a ridge.

Walker had continued to cover my left with his skirmishers, but he now rejoined the brigade and formed his regiment on its left flank.

The brigade had advanced about a half or three quarters of a mile very rapidly, after coming upon the enemy's cavalry, and time was given it to breathe a few minutes.

A fence enclosing the field in our front, and beside which the farm road ran, was then pulled down, and the brigade advanced into the field to the crest of a low ridge, when a considerable body of the enemy's cavalry was discovered drawn up on the ridge on the opposite side of the wheatfield, in front of a body of woods on that ridge; and at the same time three batteries of artillery opened from behind the crest of the same ridge, and in our front.

No infantry had yet been seen, but it was manifest, from the boldness with which the cavalry confronted us, and the opening of the batteries, that there must be a heavy force of infantry concealed by the ridge in our front, and I therefore halted the brigade, and made the men cover themselves as well as they could, by moving a few steps to the rear and lying down. I then sent a request to General Winder to move up.

The position which I now occupied, was in an uncultivated field in Mrs. Crittenden's farm. Immediately on my right, but a little advanced, was a clump of cedars, on the most elevated part of the ground, from which point there was a slope, to the right, to low fields or bottoms on the branch of Cedar Run, all the country between us and the base of the mountain, the northern extremity of which was opposite my right, consisting of cleared fields. On my left was the body of woods beside which the road ran, and in front of this woods was the wheatfield, with the shocks of wheat still standing, in the hollow between the two ridges and at the upper end of that hollow. Immediately in my front the ground sloped down to a small drain running from the wheatfield across the road, and beyond that drain was the cornfield.

On the left of the road, where it crossed the ridge in my front, was the body of woods in front of which the cavalry was drawn up, but there was none on the right of the road.

Immediately after sending back for Winder, I sent for some artillery, but my request had been anticipated, and Captain Brown of the Chesapeake Artillery, with one gun from his battery, and Captain Dement of the 1st Maryland Battery, with three guns, soon came dashing up through the fields, and were posted near the clump of cedars. They immediately opened on the enemy's cav-

alry and artillery, causing the former to retire speedily, through
the woods over the ridge. General Winder, moving by flank along
the road, soon came up with his advance, and some of the guns of
Jackson's division were brought into action, near the point where
the road emerges from the woods, under the supervision of Major
Andrews, chief of artillery for the division. Ewell had by this
time reached the plateau on the northern slope of the mountain,
and caused two batteries with him to open also on the enemy.

I had posted a regiment, the 12th Georgia, on the right of
Brown's and Dement's guns to protect them, as there was a wide
uncovered space between them and Ewell's position on the mountain.

The cannonade had now become very brisk, and I discovered
that one of the enemy's batteries had been compelled to change
its position.

As the brigades under Winder came up, they were moved into
the woods confronting the wheatfield on the left of the road. Being
in a position to observe the nature of the ground in front, I sent
the information to General Winder that, by moving a force around
the upper end of the wheatfield, and through the woods on the
opposite ridge, he could get on the flank of the enemy's batteries.
In a few moments, however, I discovered, by the glistening of the
muskets and bayonets in that wood, though the men could'nt be
seen, that the enemy was stealthily sending an infantry force to our
left, and I immediately sent a staff officer to inform General Winder of the fact, and caution him to look out for his left flank. My
messenger found that that gallant officer had just been mortally
wounded by a shell, and the message was delivered to General
Jackson in person, he having arrived on the field.

General Wm. B. Taliaferro now succeeded to the command of
the three brigades of Jackson's division that were up. Taliaferro's
own brigade, now commanded by Colonel Taliaferro, was immediately on my left—Jones's brigade, under Colonel Garnett, was
on the left of Taliaferro's, facing the wheatfield, with its left extending to another narrow field running back from the wheatfield.
Winder's brigade, the Stonewall, under Colonel Ronald, was in
reserve in rear of Garnett's left.

When the artillery fire had continued about two hours after the
enemy's batteries first opened on my brigade, I discovered his in-

fantry advancing in line through the cornfield, preceded by a line of skirmishers, but it halted and lay down before getting within musket range, being partially concealed by the growing corn which was more than head-high. This line of infantry overlapped my right flank, and I sent a request to General Jackson for a brigade to post on that flank, and it was promised. Before it arrived, however, two batteries attached to Hill's divison, Pegram's and Fleet's, which came upon the field in advance of the division, suddenly dashed to the front of the left of my brigade, and commenced unlimbering within musket range of the enemy's skirmishers, which, with the line in rear, immediately arose and advanced firing. Seeing that the guns would be captured or disabled, unless supported immediately, I ordered my brigade forward at a double-quick, and it arrived just in time to save the guns. About this time, Major Snowden Andrews, while moving some of the guns of Jackson's division to an advanced position, received a frightful wound from a bursting shell, which the surgeons pronounced mortal, but the Major determined to live, and did live and recover in spite of the doctors.

As soon as the safety of Hill's batteries was secured, the 12th Georgia was moved up, and posted on the crest of a small ridge leading out from the main one and around in front of the clump of cedars, so as to have an oblique flank fire on the enemy immediately in front of the brigade. Large bodies of infantry had now advanced through the wheatfield, and against Garnett's extreme left, and the engagement became general along the front, and raged with great fury. Just as I had posted the 12th Georgia on the right of my brigade, Thomas's Georgia brigade of Hill's division, having arrived in advance of the division, came to my assistance, by General Jackson's order as promised, and I proceeded to post it on the right of the 12th Georgia, on the extension of the same ridge, so as to confront the force overlapping my right. While doing this the left and centre of my own brigade were concealed from my view, and on riding back I found that the batteries of Hill's division to the support of which my brigade had gone, were moving to the rear, and the left and centre regiments were falling back obliquely from the woods on their left. I at once ordered a staff officer to gallop to the retiring regiments and bring them back,

The 12th Georgia, four companies of the 52nd Virginia, and a portion of the 58th Virginia were still holding their position on the right, and I rode to them and urged their commanders to hold their ground at all hazards, as other troops would soon come to our assistance. Captain Wm. F. Brown, commanding the 12th Georgia, replied very promptly: "General, my ammunition is nearly exhausted, don't you think I had better charge them?" I could but be struck with admiration at the coolness and determination of the old man, for he was then sixty five years of age, but I said to him: "Captain, if we can hold on until other troops come up we will do very well." And here I must relate something of the history of Captain Brown. He had been with General Ned Johnson at Alleghany Mountains, and with General Jackson in his Valley campaign, from McDowell to Port Republic, but he had then resigned. A few days before the battle of Cedar Run, he reported to me for duty, and told me that, after the termination of the Valley campaign, he had concluded that, as he was old and had a son who was first Lieutenant of his company, it was his duty to go home and look after the old woman (as he termed her) and the rest of the children—so he had sent in his resignation and got a leave of absence.

He then went home and stayed about two weeks, but, he said: "General, I saw so many young men lying around doing nothing, when they ought to be in the army, that I swore, I'd be d——d if I would stay among them—so I came back to Richmond, withdrew my resignation, and I have come to report to you for duty."

There being no field-officer present with the regiment, he, being the senior captain, was put in command of the 12th Georgia. If I had given the word he would have charged the whole force in our front, and the 12th Georgia would promptly have obeyed his order, for it never did know how to refuse to fight. I will add that his regiment was not long afterwards transferred to Trimble's brigade, and when General Trimble was wounded on the 29th of August, Captain Brown, as the senior officer present, succeeded to the command of the brigade, though only a captain; and he was killed at Ox Hill in command of it, on the 1st of September. No braver or truer man fell during the entire war.

Returning from this episode to the battle I was describing, I will state that my brigade, with the assistance of the guns of Brown and Dement as well as those of Pegram and Fleet, which rendered very efficient service with cannister, had kept the enemy at bay in the cornfield; but, farther to the left, the enemy had attacked very fiercely Garnett's front, while a heavy force was thrown upon his left, compelling it to give way. The enemy then got in his rear, and the whole brigade was forced to retire, when the attacking force assailed the left and rear of Taliaferro's brigade in the woods, which likewise gave way, but not until Colonel Taliaferro had made an obstinate resistance with the regiments on the right of the brigade. He was, however, compelled to order those regiments to fall back also. The enemy, now having possession of the woods on the left of my brigade, opened fire on that flank, while it was exposed to another in front. The centre regiments first gave way, but Colonel Walker still maintained his position, with his own regiment and a portion of the 31st Virginia, in support of the batteries, until all the pieces were carried off safely, and the enemy had penetrated into the field in his rear. He then ordered his regiment and the portion of the 31st with him, to fall back obliquely from the woods. It was just at this crisis that I came in view of that part of the field after posting Thomas.

The latter held his position firmly on the right, keeping the enemy's left in check, while pouring a destructive fire into its ranks. The 12th Georgia, the four companies of the 52nd, and the portion of the 58th, still held their ground, Brown's and Dement's guns continuing a destructive fire of cannister into the enemy in front of those commands—Captains Brown and Dement themselves serving their pieces when their men were exhausted. Very soon, Branch's, Archer's and Pender's brigades of Hill's division arrived, and were moved forward on the left of the road, speedily clearing the woods of the enemy—Winder's brigade, under Colonel Ronald, gallantly and efficiently co-operating. The retiring regiments of my brigade were soon rallied and returned to the front, as was the case also with Taliaferro's brigade.

Just as Hill's brigades had reached the edge of the wheatfield, in the pursuit of the now retreating enemy, and Taliaferro's brigade and my regiments were pressing forward on their right, the enemy made a desperate effort to retrieve the fortunes of the day by a cavalry charge. Suddenly a body of cavalry came charging over the ridge and along the road, getting to within forty or fifty steps of General Taliaferro and myself, who were directing our respective commands, when the men, without attempting any formation, pour-

ed a volley into the head of the charging column, which caused it
to turn abruptly to its right, through the wheatfield, when it received raking volleys from Hill's brigades, as it ran the gauntlet,
by which many saddles were emptied.  This ended the contest and
our troops pressed on in pursuit.  The troops in front of Thomas
were the last to give way, but they soon followed the retreating
masses.

It was now nearly night, but our troops continued to pursue the
enemy, Field's brigade, and a Louisiana brigade, under Colonel
Stafford, of Hill's division, which arrived just as the action closed,
taking the lead.

The pursuit was continued about a mile and a half, when fresh
troops of the enemy were encountered, which had just arrived.
There was some artillery firing at this point, but the pursuit now
ceased, as it had become dark, and Colonel Wm. E. Jones, in
pressing to the front with his regiment, the 7th Virginia Cavalry,
had captured the negro servant of a Federal officer, from whom it
was ascertained that Sigel's corps had arrived.  There was therefore a halt for the night.

Trimble's and Hays's brigades had not been engaged, but the
two batteries, which Ewell had on the plateau on the mountain,
and were supported by those brigades, had rendered efficient
service.

General Ewell had not been able to advance against the enemy
during the engagement, by reason of the artillery fire from our
batteries, which swept the valley in his front; but when the retreat
of the enemy began, he moved down and joined the main column
before the pursuit ended.

The troops we had engaged and defeated were those of Banks's
corps mainly, but before the action or rather the pursuit closed,
Pope arrived with Rickett's division of McDowell's corps, which,
he says, "just at dusk, came up and joined in the engagement."
Rickett's division numbered over 8,000 men.   Sigel's corps arrived
subsequently

We had only eight brigades actually engaged, to wit: three of
Jackson's division, four of Hill's, and my own.   Ewell, however,
was within supporting distance with two others.   Lawton's brigade
of Jackson's division and Gregg's brigade of Hill's division were
in the rear guarding the trains, which the enemy's cavalry was re-

ported to be threatening. Field's and Stafford's brigades did not arrive until the close of the action, and a part of my brigade was absent on picket duty as before stated.

A reconnoissance made next morning by the cavalry, under the charge of General Stuart, who had arrived on a tour of inspection, disclosed the fact that the greater part of Pope's army had arrived, and the rest was coming up.

General Jackson, therefore, did not deem it prudent to push on. There was some artillery firing that morning at long range, but in the afternoon we fell back to the vicinity of the battlefield. On the next day, Pope sent a flag of truce, requesting permission to bury his dead, and carry off his wounded, and it was granted until two o'clock, P. M., but subsequently extended, until all his dead were buried.

I was on the field in person during the existence of the truce, and the greater part of the enemy's dead were taken from the cornfield in front of the positions occupied by my brigade and Thomas's. I had, on that day, with details from my own brigade, ninety-eight of our dead buried, which were found in the woods where Jackson's division had fought, and had been overlooked by their proper commands. I also had six wagon loads of small arms, that the enemy had left on the field, carried to the rear. They had been stacked by the command assigned to that duty, the day before, but had not been carried off, though a larger number had been sent to the rear. The enemy on this day, buried something over six hundred dead that were lying on the field.

On the night of the 11th, we began retiring to the rear, and returned to our former positions near Gordonsville, on the 13th. We captured one piece of artillery, and something over five thousand stand of small arms.

Our loss was, in killed 223, wounded 1,060, and missing 31—in all 1,314.

Pope does not give in numbers his loss, but says it was heavy. He had now seen something more of the "rebels" than their backs, and was destined soon to behold other new and more startling sights.

In his official report, he says:

"The consolidated report of General Banks's corps, received some days previously, exhibited an effective force of something over fourteen thousand men. Appended herewith will be found the return in question. It appeared subsequently, however, that General Banks's forces at that time did not exceed eight thousand men. But although I several times called General Banks's attention to the discrepancy between this return and the force he afterwards stated to me he had led to front, that discrepancy has never been explained and I do not yet understand how General Banks could have been so greatly mistaken as to the forces under his command."

Then follows the return, as follows :

|  | INFANTRY. | ARTILLERY. | CAVALRY. | TOTAL. |
|---|---|---|---|---|
| "1st Army Corps [Sigel's] | 10,550 | 948 | 1,730 | 13,228 |
| 2d Army Corps [Banks's] | 13,343 | 1,224 | 4,104 | 18,671 |
| 3d Army Corps [McDowell's] | 17,604 | 971 | 2,904 | 21,479 |
| Total, | 41,497 | 3,143 | 8,738 | 53,378 |
| Deduct infantry brigade stationed at Winchester, |  |  | 2,500 |  |
| Deduct regiment and battery at Front Royal, |  |  | 1,000 |  |
| Deduct cavalry unfit for service, |  |  | 3,000 |  |
|  |  |  |  | 6,500 |
| Total, |  |  |  | 47,878 |

I certify that this is a true copy of the consolidated morning report of the Army of Virginia, dated July 31st, 1862, commanded by Major General Pope."

"MYER ASCH, *Captain and Aide-de-Camp.*"

Pope seems to be surprised that Banks could not explain the discrepancy about his strength, between his official return and his statement after he had fought Jackson at Cedar Run. The fact is that Banks's mind always did become confused when Stonewall Jackson was about. In his report, Pope further says: "The day of the 10th was intensely hot, and the troops on both sides were too much fatigued to renew the action. My whole effective force on that day, exclusive of Banks's corps, which was in no condition for service, was about twenty thousand artillery and infantry, and about two thousand cavalry; General Buford with the cavalry force under his command, not yet having been able to join the main body."

King's division of McDowell's corps came up on the evening of the 11th, and Pope then had his entire army concentrated. It will thus be seen that it was a very prudent step on General Jackson's part to retire on the night of the 11th.

It is hard to tell what it was that prevented Buford from joining the main body. On the 8th, he sent a dispatch, by signal, from Madison C. H., to Banks, which is given by Pope as follows: "All of my force is withdrawn from Madison Court House, and is in retreat toward Sperryville. The enemy is in force on both my right and left, and in my rear. I may be cut off."

I can't conceive what it was that scared him so badly. Robertson, with all his brigade except one regiment, was driving another body of the enemy's cavalry across Robertson River on the 8th. The 6th Virginia Cavalry and White's company moved in the direction of Madison C. H. on the 7th, and separately encountered portions of the enemy's cavalry which they drove before them. Perhaps, it was this regiment and company which alarmed Buford.

The very presence of General Jackson in the vicinity of Gordonsville had bewildered the minds, and excited anew the fears of the authorities at Washington; and on the 3d of August the peremptory order was given for the evacuation of Harrison's Landing, and the re-inforcement of Pope by McClellan's army. In his reply to some questions propounded by the committee on the conduct of the war, in May 1865, Pope said:

"Jackson was at Gordonsville on the 4th of August, the day that General McClellan received orders to withdraw from the Peninsula; and the battle of Cedar Mountain was fought on the 9th of August, by the three corps under Jackson his own, Ewell's and A. P. Hill's, supported by Longstreet's corps behind the Rapidan."

On the 6th of August, Halleck, in a letter to McClellan, said:

"You and your officers at our interview estimated the enemy's forces in and around Richmond at two hundred thousand men. Since then, you and others report that they have received and are receiving large re-inforcements from the South. General Pope's army, covering Washington is only about forty thousand. Your effective force is only about ninety thousand. You are thirty miles from Richmond, and General Pope eighty or ninety, with the enemy directly between you ready to fall with his superior numbers upon one or the other as he may elect; neither can re-inforce the other in case of such an attack."

On the 9th he telegraphed McClellan:

"I am of the opinion the enemy is massing his forces in front of Generals Pope and Burnside, and that he expects to crush them and move forward to the Potomac. You must send re-inforcements instantly to Aquia Creek"

After the battle of Cedar Run, the spectre of "overwhelming numbers" at Richmond, and a speedy advance on Washington, assumed a fearful shape, and Halleck became frantic in his directions to McClellan to hasten the evacuation, and send forward re-inforcements to avert the threatened disaster. Burnside, with 13,000 men from the coast of North Carolina, on his way to join McClellan, had previously been diverted from that destination and sent to the vicinity of Fredericksburg.

On the 14th in response to Halleck, McClellan telegraphed:

"Movement has commenced by land and water. All sick will be away to-morrow night. Every thing done to carry out your orders. I don't like Jackson's movements; he will suddenly appear when least expected."

There were none on that side who did like Jackson's movements, when he was on the war-path; and on this occasion he certainly caused Richmond to be entirely relieved of the danger of a threatened siege, not to be renewed for the period of two years, and until he himself was in his grave.

On the 14th of August, Reno, with 8,000 men of Burnside's corps joined Pope's army.

## ADVANCE AGAINST POPE.

Having ascertained that McClellan was sending troops to re-inforce Pope, General Lee, on the 13th, ordered General Longstreet, with his division, D. R. Jones's division, two brigades under General Hood, and Evans's brigade to Gordonsville. General Stuart was ordered to the same vicinity with Fitz Lee's brigade of cavalry, and General R. H. Anderson was ordered to follow Longstreet with his division. Longstreet having arrived, General Jackson's command was moved in the direction of Somerville Ford on the Rapidan, on the 15th, and camped three or four miles from the ford. The command had not been increased since the battle of Cedar Run, but Lawton's brigade had been transferred to Ewell's division, and the Louisiana brigade, previously under Colonel Stafford but now under General Starke, had been transferred from Hill's division to Jackson's. A day or two before the 20th, the 49th Virginia, under Colonel Wm. Smith, joined my brigade, and this constituted the sole accession to General Jackson's command; but it did not number one-third of the loss at Cedar Run.

General Lee having arrived and assumed command, a forward movement was commenced on the 20th, which was to have begun on the 18th; but Pope, having learned the intended movement from a dispatch to Stuart, which was captured by a party of the enemy's cavalry, hastily retired across the Rappahannock. On the 20th, General Jackson crossed at Somerville Ford, and bivouacked for the night near Stevensburg in Culpeper County. He was preceded by three regiments of Robertson's cavalry brigade, accompanied by General Stuart in person. On the same day Longstreet, preceded by Fitz Lee's brigade of cavalry, crossed lower down at Raccoon Ford, and moved to the vicinity of Kelley's Ford on the Rappahannock. Robertson's cavalry encountered a superior force of the enemy's cavalry near Brandy Station, which was driven across the Rappahannock, after a sharp engagement. Fitz Lee also encountered a force of cavalry at Kelley's Ford, and drove it across the river.

On the 21st, General Jackson moved past Brandy Station to Beverly's Ford on the Rappahannock, at which point, Stuart, who preceded the infantry column with Robertson's brigade and two regiments of Fitz Lee's, under Colonel Rosser, sent Rosser across with his two regiments, and Robertson crossed subsequently at a ford farther up. There was heavy artillery firing here across the river from both sides, but the enemy appearing on the opposite bank in large force, it was determined to seek a crossing farther to our left—Rosser and Robertson having been withdrawn on the approach of the enemy in force.

On the next day, the 22nd, General Jackson crossed Hazel River and moved to a point opposite the Fauquier Sulphur Springs, Ewell's division being in the advance; but Trimble's brigade was left near the crossing of Hazel River to protect the trains as they passed. In the meantime Longstreet had moved up from Kelley's Ford, in order to cover the ford at the rail-road bridge and the crossings above, so as to mask General Jackson's movement to the left. Taliaferro had been left with Jackson's division to cover Beverly's Ford until relieved, and there was again some cannonading at that point across the river in the morning. In the afternoon, a considerable force of the enemy which had crossed at Freeman's Ford, above the junction of the two streams, was attacked by Trimble's brigade, supported by Hood's two brigades, which had arrived to relieve it, and, after a severe conflict, Trimble succeeded in driving the enemy across the river with severe loss.

Late in the afternoon, the 13th Georgia regiment of Lawton's brigade, and Brown's and Dement's batteries were crossed over the river at the Sulphur Springs, a small force of cavalry having retired on our advance, after destroying the bridge. My own brigade was crossed over about a mile lower down, and moved to the front, where I took position in a body of pine woods. I was told that Lawton would cross with his whole brigade at the Springs, and I was directed to communicate with him. It was intended that Hays's brigade should cross at the same point at which I crossed, but before I got over it was nearly night, and the crossing of that brigade was deferred until the next morning. It was dark before my brigade was in position and pickets thrown out. I found on my left a road leading through the woods from Rappahannock Station to the Springs, and as soon as my dispositions were made I sent a volunteer aide, Major A. L. Pitzer, to find General Lawton at the Springs. It was now quite dark; there had been a heavy shower in the afternoon, and the muttering of thunder and flashing of lightning foretold a storm. On reaching the vicinity of the Springs, the Major came upon a party of cavalry-men, a sergeant and five privates, to whom his presence was disclosed by the flash of the lightning. He was immediately made a prisoner and disarmed, when this party, which passed up the road just before my arrival, started back with him; but he so worked upon their fears that he brought in the whole party as prisoners, with their horses, arms and equipments. This incident prevented any further effort to communicate with General Lawton that night.

During the night, the threatened storm burst upon us, and the rain poured down in torrents. At light next morning I discovered the Rappahannock out of its banks, and I found myself cut off from the rest of the army except the force at the Springs. In a short time I received a verbal message from General Jackson, by a sergeant of one of the batteries at the Springs, which had been communicated across the river; and by this I was directed to move up to the Springs, take command of all the forces there, and make preparations for defence. I was also informed that only the 13th Georgia, under Colonel Douglas, of Lawton's brigade, had crossed over at the Springs ; and that General Jackson was having the bridge repaired, and would have it in condition for infantry to pass over as soon as possible.

I had previously sent a note to General Ewell or General Jackson, whichever should be first met with, suggesting that my brigade and the force at the Springs be moved up the river to Waterloo bridge, to escape capture, which seemed to be inevitable under the circumstances. This had been sent by a messenger with directions to him to swim the river, and, after the delivery of the verbal message, I received a note from General Jackson, in reply to mine, in which the verbal instructions were repeated, and I was further directed, if the enemy appeared in too heavy force for me, to move up the river along the bank to Waterloo bridge, with the assurance that he would follow on the other side with his whole force and protect me with his artillery. I moved up to the Springs as soon as practicable, and posted my brigade in a woods, a short distance below, near which Colonel Douglas had already posted his regiment and the batteries. I found, north of the Springs, a stream called Great Run, which emptied into the Rappahannock below my position of the night before, and that was also impassible, it being fortunately between us and the enemy. A bridge over it, which was partially flooded, had been destroyed by Colonel Douglas, and we were safe for a time at least. Only a small body of cavalry had at that time made its appearance on the opposite side of this stream. In order to prevent surprise from below, two regiments were posted on the road from that direction, and we awaited events with great anxiety, as a matter of course. My greatest apprehension was of a movement of the enemy from the direction of Warrenton, but fortunately he had no force there at that juncture. It took longer to repair the bridge than had been expected, and in the meantime Great Run had fallen rapidly, and in the afternoon was in a condition to be crossed. The enemy was now moving up from below in heavy force, on a road that ran beyond Great Run towards Warrenton, his trains and troops being partially visible to us. My command was entirely concealed from the enemy by the woods in which it was posted, but it was evident that he was aware of the fact that a force was on that side of the river, and from the caution with which he moved he must have thought it very much larger than it really was.

The day before, Stuart, with his cavalry, had crossed at Waterloo Bridge above, and made a raid at night into Pope's head-quarter train near Catlett's Station—he did not however get into his saddle.

He captured what was supposed to be Pope's uniform, and his dispatch book, besides making captures of horses and prisoners, and then retired in safety after having created great dismay and confusion. Fortunately for us, he did not capture General Pope himself. The consternation produced by this raid doubtless contributed very greatly to the safety of my command in its isolated position.

Late in the afternoon, a heavy column of infantry, accompanied by artillery, made its appearance on the heights opposite my right flank. About this time, General Robertson, who had been on the raid with Stuart, arrived with two or three of his regiments and two pieces of artillery, from the direction of Warrenton, and his pieces were posted on a ridge north of the Springs, and opened on the enemy. This fire was responded to by some of the enemy's guns, and I had two Parrot guns of Brown's battery sent to the assistance of Robertson's guns, when a brisk cannonade ensued which lasted until near sunset. Care had been taken to post these guns so far to my left, that the fire directed at them could not affect my infantry.

After this artillery firing ceased, a column of the enemy's infantry advanced to the bank of Great Run, just in front of the right of the woods in which my brigade was posted, and other bodies of infantry were discovered moving around to the left, though barely visible through the mist and approaching darkness.

The column that had reached Great Run, moved up and formed line in front of the woods where my brigade was, and after giving three cheers and a tiger in regular style, poured a volley into the woods. Two of Dement's Napoleons were immediately run out beyond my left, and opened with cannister on the enemy, causing him to change his tune very suddenly. The fire from Dement's guns had to be directed by the noise the enemy made, as the atmosphere was hazy and it was getting dark. It was so well directed, however, that the force that made the advance was thrown into confusion, and soon retired. It was now evident that my command was confronted by a very heavy force, and that preparations were being made to surround it.

Another of Lawton's regiments had by this time crossed over on the bridge, which had been partially repaired. I sent a messenger to Generals Ewell and Jackson to inform them of the condition of things, and the rest of Lawton's brigade was crossed over after n'ght. When General Lawton himself arrived, about 1 o'clock at night, he informed me that General Jackson had instructed General Ewell to cross over himself at daylight, and if it was evident that a heavy force was confronting me, to withdraw the two brigades, as it was not desired to have a general engagement at that place. On hearing this, I immediately dispatched a messenger to Ewell, to inform him that there was no doubt about the size of the enemy's force, and if we were to be withdrawn, the withdrawal had better begin at once, as by day-break the enemy would, in all probability, have artillery in position to command the bridge, the sound of moving wheels around to my left indicating some such purpose. A little after three o'clock, General Ewell came over, and after consultation with Generals Lawton and myself, gave the necessary orders for our withdrawal, though very reluctantly, as he insisted the enemy was retreating. Lawton's brigade went first, carrying over the artillery by hand, and my brigade followed just as it became fairly light.

As Ewell and myself rode off in rear of my brigade, the enemy's infantry was discovered advancing in line, with skirmishers in front, and the corps of Sigel, Banks, and Reno soon passed over the very ground we had occupied, and took position near the Springs. A heavy artillery duel then ensued between the batteries of the enemy and those of Hill's division which continued for some hours. In the afternoon, Sigel pursued an imaginary foe in the direction of Waterloo Bridge, as all of our cavalry as well as the infantry and artillery had recrossed the river in safety.

On the 21st, Halleck telegraphed Pope:

"I have just sent General Burnside's reply. General Cox's forces are coming in from Parkersburg, and will be here to-morrow and next day. Dispute every inch of ground, and fight like the devil until we can re-inforce you. Forty-eight hours more and we can make you strong enough. Don't yield an inch if you can help it."

On the 23d Pope telegraphed Halleck :

"The enemy's forces on this side, which have crossed at Sulphur Springs and Hedgeman's river, are cut off from those on the other side. I march at once with my whole force on Sulphur Springs, Waterloo bridge, and Warrenton, with the hope to destroy these forces before the river runs down."

On the 24th, at 3.45 P. M., he wrote Halleck :

"I arrived in Warrenton last night : the enemy had left two hours previously. Milroy's brigade, the advance of Sigel's corps, came upon the enemy late yesterday afternoon near Great Run, about four miles from Warrenton Sulphur Springs, and near the mouth of it. A sharp action took place, which lasted till dark, the enemy being driven across Great Run, but destroying the bridge behind him. * * Sigel's forces advanced again on the left this morning, and when last heard from was pursuing the enemy in the direction of Waterloo bridge. * * * No force of the enemy has yet been able to cross, except that now enclosed by our forces between Sulphur Springs and Waterloo bridge, which will no doubt be captured, unless they find some means, of which I know nothing, of escaping across the river between these places."

From these extracts, it will be seen in what a critical position I had been, and how well Pope understood the condition of things.

On the 23d, some of Longstreet's batteries, supported by two brigades of infantry, had forced a body of the enemy that were across the river at Rappahannock Station, to recross at that point over a pontoon bridge, which was destroyed by the enemy ; and on the 24th, the river still being impassable, Longstreet's whole force had moved up to the support of General Jackson's command.

The dispatch book captured by Stuart disclosed the fact that McClellan's army had evacuated Harrison's Landing, that a portion of it had already joined Pope, that the remainder was being sent to him over the Orange and Alexandria rail-road, and that Cox's troops from the Kanawha Valley were being brought over the Baltimore and Ohio rail-road for the same purpose. General Lee, therefore, determined to send General Jackson to the rear of

Pope, to break the rail-road and thus separate him from the approaching re-inforcements, and to follow with Longstreet's command as soon as General Jackson was well on his way.

## MOVEMENT TO POPE'S REAR.

The necessary orders having been given the day before, early on the morning of the 25th, General Jackson moved with his command to Hinson's Mill, some miles above Waterloo Bridge, and crossed the river, called here Hedgeman's River. Then moving by Orlean, the command reached the vicinity of Salem in Fauquier County, and bivouacked for the night. All baggage wagons had been left behind, and no vehicles were allowed except ordnance and hospital wagons, and ambulances, the men carrying three days' cooked rations in their haversacks. The 2d Virginia cavalry, under Colonel Munford, preceded the command, picketing the side roads as the column passed on. Resuming the march early on the 26th, we passed White Plains, moved through Thoroughfare Gap in the Bull Run Mountain, and passing Haymarket, reached Gainesville, where the Manassas Gap rail-road crosses the Warrenton turnpike. Stuart, with the rest of the cavalry of Fitz Lee's and Robertson's brigades, overtook us here in the afternoon, having very early that morning left the south bank of the Rappahannock, and followed General Jackson's route. From this point, the column moved towards Bristoe Station on the rail-road, preceded by Munford's regiment, which was followed by Hays's brigade, Ewell's division being in the advance. Stuart's cavalry moved on the flank so as to protect the column from surprise or attack from the direction of the Rappahannock or Warrenton. Munford reached the station near night and found it guarded by a company of cavalry and a company of infantry. The cavalry galloped off, but the infantry took to the houses, and while Munford's command was skirmishing with it, a train approached from the direction of the Rappahannock, which he endeavored to stop or throw from the track by placing cross-ties in front, but the train ran over all obstacles, and escaped in the direction of Manassas. Hays's brigade, under Colonel Forno, soon arrived, and two other trains that were following were stopped and captured by it. Munford captured some prisoners and horses. The attention of General Jackson was now directed to the stores and munitions at Manassas, about four miles from Bristoe, where it was learned a large supply had been collected. In regard to its capture, I give General Jackson's own words—He says: "Notwithstanding the darkness of the night, and the fatiguing march which would, since dawn, be over thirty miles, before reaching the Junction, Brigadier General Trimble volunteered to proceed there forthwith, with the 21st North Carolina (Lieutenant Colonel Fulton commanding) and 21st Georgia (Major Glover commanding), in all, about 500 men, and capture the place. I accepted the gallant offer, and gave him orders to move without delay. In order to increase the prospect of success, Major General Stuart, with a portion of his cavalry, was subsequently directed to move forward, and, as the ranking officer, to take command of the expedition. This duty was cheerfully undertaken by all who were assigned to it, and most promptly and successfully executed. Notwithstanding the Federal fire of musketry and artillery, our infantry dispersed the troops placed there for the defense of the place, and captured eight guns, with seventy-two horses, equipments, and ammunition complete, immense supplies of commissary and quartermaster stores, upwards of two hundred tents; and General Trimble also reports the capture of over three hundred prisoners, and one hundred and seventy-five horses, exclusive of those belonging to the artillery, besides recovering over two hundred negroes." On the next day, the 27th, General Trimble occupied, with his brigade, the works constructed by our troops the year before.

Ewell's division had reached Bristoe Station very late, and as soon as the place was secured and the trains captured, the three brigades left after Trimble was detached, were posted so as to cover the approaches along the rail road from the direction of Warrenton Junction. The other divisions, Hill's and Jackson's, bivouacked in the vicinity, and next morning were moved to the Junction. Soon after their arrival, a body of the enemy's infantry arrived on a train from Alexandria, and having gotten off the train, moved towards the Junction for the purpose of driving off the "raiding party." It was met by the fire of two batteries and several brigades of Hill's division, and driven back and pursued for some distance, the train on which it arrived being captured and destroyed, as was the rail-road bridge over Bull Run.

Ewell had been left at Bristoe Station, with Lawton's, Hays's, and my brigades, to guard the approach from the direction of Warrenton Junction; but with instructions to retire in the direction of Manassas if a superior force advanced against him, as it was not desired to bring on a general engagement at that point. Lawton's brigade was posted on the left of the rail-road in advance of the station, Hays's on the right of it, and mine to the right of Hays's, but retired so as to be in echelon with it. The batteries were posted so as to command the front and flanks. Rosser, with his regiment of cavalry, was on out-post duty on our right flank. Colonel Forno, with some of his regiments, was sent on the morning of this day, to destroy the bridge over Kettle Run and tear up the rail-road back towards the Station. He found a train of cars beyond Kettle Run, which had just brought up a body of infantry, but a few shots from a piece of artillery he had with him, soon sent the train back. He then left one regiment on picket in front, and set another to tearing up the track of the rail-road.

It was thus that, while Pope had been resolutely looking to the front, without thought for his line of retreat or base of supplies, General Jackson had suddenly got on his line of retreat and cut him off from his base of supplies. As may well be conceived, this state of things created great confusion at Pope's head-quarters, and great consternation and dismay at Washington.

Pope at first supposed it was a mere cavalry raid in small force, and caused one of his aides to send to Heintzelman, who had now joined him, the following order: "The Major General commanding the army of Virginia directs me to send you the enclosed communication, and to request that you put a regiment on a train of cars and send it down immediately to Manassas, to ascertain what has occurred, repair the telegraph wires, and protect the rail-road there until further orders."

He was, however, soon undeceived, and thought perhaps it would be well to pay some attention to *his* own line of retreat, and leave *ours* to take care of itself. He had now a very forcible illustration of the truth of his own declaration, that "disaster and shame lurk in the rear."

Reynolds's division of Pennsylvania Reserves, and Heintzelman's and Porter's corps from McClellan's army, and Piatt's brigade of Sturgis's division from Washington, had joined Pope

before this time. Other troops had evidently arrived, for in a
letter to Halleck, dated the 25th, Pope said: "The troops arriving
here come in fragments. Am I to assign them to brigades and
corps? I would suppose not, as several of the new regiments
coming have been assigned to army corps directly from your
office."

In his official report, he says:

"As was to be expected, under such circumstances, the numbers of the army under my command had been greatly reduced
by death, by wounds, by sickness, and by fatigue, so that, on the
morning of the 27th of August, I estimated my whole effective
force (and I think the estimate was large) as follows: Sigel's
corps, nine thousand; Banks's corps, five thousand; McDowell's
corps, including Reynolds's division, fifteen thousand five hundred; Reno's corps, seven thousand; the corps of Heintzelman
and Porter (the freshest, by far, in that army,) about eighteen
thousand men; making in all fifty-four thousand five hundred
men. Our cavalry numbered, on paper, about four thousand;
but their horses were completely broken down, and there were
not five hundred men, all told, capable of doing such service as
should be expected from cavalry."

His own official return of the 31st of July had shown 41,140 infantry and artillery present for duty on that day, after the deduction for the troops at Winchester and Front Royal, and Reno had
joined him with 8,000 men, making 49,140. Piatt's brigade numbered 3,500, according to Pope's testimony on the trial of General
Porter; Reynolds's division numbered 2,500 when it joined him;
and putting Heintzelman's and Porter's corps at 18,000—though,
on the 20th of July, according to McClellan's official return of that
day, they numbered 37,353 aggregate for duty—and Pope's force
of infantry and artillery should have been 73,140 effectives, without counting the new regiments he mentions. There must, therefore, have been a loss of 18,640. Of that loss, 6,400 may be attri-
buted to the confused state of Banks's mind, and, I presume, 3,000
more to the loss at Cedar Run. What became of the balance?

His cavalry, on the 31st of July, numbered 8,738, with 3,000
unfit for service; but it now numbered only 4,000 on paper, with
3,500 unfit for cavalry service. What had become of the other
4,738?

I can't understand how the Federal armies always numbered so large on paper, and so small in the field, as was generally the case according to their commanders.

In the afternoon of the 27th, a considerable force, which came up from the direction of Warrenton Junction, and proved to be Hooker's division of Heintzelman's corps, moved across Kettle Run against our advanced regiments at Bristoe. One or two columns, apparently of brigades, were driven back, when the enemy commenced moving towards our right, over open ground beyond the range of our guns, and the force which came in view was evidently much larger than the force Ewell then had.

He, therefore, in accordance with his instructions, ordered a withdrawal, and directed me to cover that withdrawal with my brigade. Lawton's and Hays's brigades were successively withdrawn in good order, and then my brigade was withdrawn, taking successive lines of battle back to the ford on Broad Run near the rail-road bridge. Lawton's brigade had first crossed the Run and formed line of battle on the north bank, with some batteries in position, and then Hays's brigade crossed and was ordered to Manassas.

All the artillery was safely withdrawn, a part crossing at a ford several hundred yards above the bridge, where also one of my regiments crossed. My brigade was then crossed, its rear being covered by Colonel Walker's regiment deployed as skirmishers.

As soon as my brigade was over, it was moved about a mile towards Manassas, by of order General Ewell, and formed in line of battle across the road, on high ground, in full view of the enemy, whose advance had now reached the station. General Ewell then moved back through my line with Lawton's brigade, and directed me to remain in position until orders were sent to me to retire, and to move one or two of my regiments from the flanks alternately with colors elevated, so as to present the appearance of the arrival of re-inforcements.

This was done, and the enemy did not advance farther. The rail-road bridge and the captured trains had been destroyed in the morning.

Shortly after dark, under orders from General Ewell, I moved to Manassas to re-join the division.

Our loss in this affair was light ; and this is the occasion on which Pope claims that Hooker's division drove Ewell's back along the rail-road.

On arriving at the Junction, my men filled their haversacks with hard bread and salt meat, the other troops having appropriated the provisions of a more enticing character. After broiling enough of the salt meat to satisfy the hunger with which the men were oppressed, the brigade was moved out on the plains towards Blackburn's Ford on Bull Run, and bivouacked. The other brigades were bivouacked at intervals on the road to the same ford.

During the night Stuart set fire to the cars and the stores that could not be carried off, and they were destroyed, amid a terrible explosion of shells that were in some of the cars.

In the early part of the night, General Taliaferro moved with Jackson's division and all the trains of the command on the Sudley road, across the Warrenton turnpike to the vicinity of the battlefield of first Manassas, and at one o'clock at night General Hill moved with his division to Centreville. Very early on the morning of the 28th, General Ewell moved with his division across Bull Run at Blackburn's Ford, and then up the Run to the vicinity of Stone Bridge, and there crossed over and joined Jackson's division. Hill's division subsequently came up from Centreville, and the whole command was re-united north of the Warrenton turnpike, and facing it. These movements had been covered by portions of the cavalry, and were designed to mislead the enemy, in which object there was perfect success,

On the 27th, Fitz Lee, with three regiments of his brigade, went on a raid around by Fairfax C. H. to Burke's Station on the rail-road, and did not return until the afternoon of the 29th.

On the 27th, Pope commenced the movement of his troops to the rear, for the purpose of looking after his line of communications. McDowell's and Sigel's corps moved along the Warrenton turnpike in the direction of Gainesville, while the other corps moved on his right towards Manassas and Bristoe. In the meantime, Longstreet had crossed the river at Hinson's mill on the 26th, and was following the same route taken by General Jackson, Anderson, who had arrived with his division, having relieved Longstreet on the south bank of the Rappahannock. Longstreet reached White Plains on the 27th, and on the morning of the 28th his advance reached Thoroughfare Gap, where a part of McDowell's force was posted to dispute his passage.

He succeeded, however, in forcing a passage, by sending a force directly on the road through the Gap, while other troops were passed over the Mountain on the north or left of the Gap, so as to turn the flank of the enemy; and a part of his command passed through the Gap that evening.

Rosser, with his regiment, was on the south of the turnpike, watching the enemy from the direction of Manassas, and Colonel Brien with the 1st Virginia Cavalry was on the turnpike watching in the direction of Gainesville, while Colonel Bradley T. Johnson, in command of Jones's brigade of Jackson's division, was near Groveton with the brigade, picketing the turnpike in the direction of Gainesville, and a road leading from Bristoe Station across the turnpike towards Sudley. Stuart, with portions of Robertson's and Fitz Lee's brigades, this day moved to our right to Haymarket, where he had a skirmish with a body of the enemy while Long-street's troops were engaged in Thoroughfare Gap.

The main body of Pope's troops were now converging on Manassas, where he expected to find General Jackson's force and destroy it. Here is what he says in his report: " At 9 o'clock on the night of the 27th, satisfied of Jackson's position, I sent orders to General McDowell to push forward at the very earliest dawn of day towards Manassas Junction from Gainesville, resting his right on the Manassas Gap rail-road, and throwing his left well to the east. I directed General Reno to march at the same hour from Greenwich, direct upon Manassas Junction, and Kearney to march at the same hour upon Bristow. This latter order was sent to Kearney to render my right at Bristow perfectly secure against the probable movement of Jackson in that direction. Kearney arrived at Bristow about 8 o'clock in the morning. Reno being on the left, and marching direct upon Manassas Junction, I immediately pushed Kearney forward in pursuit of Ewell, towards Manassas, followed by Hooker."

But the bird he expected to trap had flown, and Pope then directed his troops to move on Centreville.

McDowell in moving towards Manassas had his left on the turn-pike, and in the forenoon the advance on that flank appeared in front of Johnson, when there was some skirmishing and fighting with it, in which artillery was used. Rosser also had some skirmishing, and used some artillery borrowed from Johnson on some trains that were discovered moving in the direction of Manassas.

The approach of the enemy having been reported to General Jackson, he made preparations for attacking him, upon the supposition that he would move along the turnpike in the direction of Centreville, but discovering, late in the afternoon, that the enemy was turning off in the direction of Manassas before reaching our front, three brigades of Jackson's division were moved to the right, through a body of woods and across a track that had been graded and excavated for a rail-road, into some fields beyond, near Brawner's house. These brigades were closely followed by Ewell's division, Lawton's and Trimble's brigades being moved, under General Ewell's immediate command, out into the fields and formed on the left of the brigades of Jackson's division, while my own brigade and Hays's were held in reserve, under my command, in the edge of the woods, with the left of each brigade near the rail-road grade, Hays's being in the rear of mine. Johnson had retired from his position near Groveton, but had not rejoined Jackson's division. The line, as now formed, was parallel to the turnpike, and just before sunset a column of the enemy commenced moving past, when the three brigades of Jackson's division and the two with Ewell advanced to the attack. And obstinate and sanguinary engagement ensued, which lasted until after dark, artillery as well as infantry being used on both sides.

At the close of the engagement, both sides maintained their ground, the enemy consisting of King's division of McDowell's corps which was bringing up the rear of McDowell's left, having been heavily re-inforced. An artillery fire was kept up for some time, but during the night King's division retired. The loss was heavy on both sides. The two brigades with me were not engaged, but were ordered to advance by General Jackson just before the close of the action, and my own brigade was exposed to a severe shelling as it moved into position near the left of Trimble's brigade. The advance on our part had ceased by this time, as the darkness, coupled with the nature of the ground in front, rendered such advance very hazardous. Rosser had taken position on Taliaferro's right, with his cavalry regiment, and rendered very efficient service. Stuart had returned from Haymarket, but did not reach the right of the line until the fighting was over. None of Hill's troops were engaged, but some of his brigades were moved up to the vicinity of the battlefield, though they did not arrive to within supporting distance until after the close of the engagement. Generals Ewell and Taliaferro were wounded, the former having to suffer amputation of a leg. General Lawton now succeeded to the command of Ewell's division, and General Starke to the command of Jackson's Division.

Early on the morning of the 29th, the enemy began to approach in heavy force from the direction of Manassas and Centreville, it having been discovered that General Jackson was not to be found at either point. To meet the approaching forces, our troops were at first moved from the positions they occupied at the close of the action the night before, and formed in line on a ridge which the rail-road grade crossed, with Ewell's division on the right, Hill's on the left, and Jackson's in the centre. In this position our line crossed the rail-road grade, with the right resting near the turnpike and the left extending towards Sudley. There was some artillery firing from the enemy, at long range, at this time. Stuart again moved out in the direction of Haymarket and Gainesville with the cavalry. As soon as the enemy's movements began to be developed, General Jackson re-arranged his line so as to conform to them. Jackson's division, under Starke, was formed on the right in the woods through which the rail-road grade ran, a little in rear of that grade. Hill's division on the left, with the brigades of Field, Thomas and Gregg in the front line on the rail-road grade, and Archer's, Pender's and Branch's in their rear as supports, and Lawton's and Trimble's brigades of Ewell's division in the centre, Trimble's brigade taking position on the rail-road grade, while Lawton's, under Colonel Douglas, was in the rear in the woods. My own and Hays's brigades, under my command, were moved about a mile to the rear of the right of the line, and posted on a ridge on the west side of a road called the Pageland road, which crosses the Warrenton turnpike. This position commanded a view of the turnpike in front and large fields between it and the turnpike as well as the Pageland road on the left. A considerable force of the enemy had been reported by the cavalry to be advancing on the road from Manassas towards Gainesville, thus threatening our right flank and rear, and my orders were to watch that force and hold it in check. A battery of artillery had accompanied my command, and was posted so as to command the ground in front, the 13th and 31st Virginia regiments being posted by General Jackson, in person, beyond the turnpike in my front, in order to apprise me of the approach of the enemy.

Longstreet's command was now known to be approaching from the direction of Thoroughfare Gap, and the object of posting me in this position was to keep open communication with him, as well as to protect our right and rear.

Several batteries from Ewell's and Jackson's divisions were posted behind the crest of the ridge, in the fields on the right of the line, and the batteries of Hill's division were posted on a ridge in some fields in rear of the left of his front line of infantry,—the nature of the ground beyond that flank over which the rail-road grade ran, rendering that grade an unsafe line to occupy, as the slope was towards Hill's position, and the grade here ran through fields.

The manœuvring of General Jackson, after he got upon Pope's line of communications to the rear, upon the approach of the enemy, furnishes an exhibition of what is known as "Grand Tactics" which is unsurpassed in the annals of war. By his movements, he had completely baffled Pope's efforts to crush him with a vastly superior force, and bewildered him as to his own locality, until he had placed his command in a strong position, where it could be joined by Longstreet's approaching forces, and the army be thus re-united under General Lee.

But Pope was not the only one that General Jackson had mystified on this occasion, and to show the bewilderment of the authorities in and about Washington, a few extracts from the official dispatches are given.

McClellan had arrived at Alexandria on the night of the 26th, and on the 27th he telegraphed Heintzelman and Porter, though the telegram was not received, perhaps :

"Where are you, and what is the state of affairs—what troops in your front, right and left? Sumner is now landing at Aquia. Where is Pope's left, and what of enemy? Enemy burned Bull Run bridge last night with cavalry force."

On the 28th, Halleck telegraphed McClellan :

"I think you had better place Sumner's corps, as it arrives, near the guns, and particularly at the Chain Bridge. The principal thing to be feared now is a cavalry raid into this city, especially in the night time. Use Cox's and Tyler's brigades, and the new troops for the same object, if you need them."

On the 29th, he telegraphed McClellan :

"Meagher's brigade ordered up yesterday. Fitzhugh Lee was, it is said on good authority, in Alexandria on Sunday last for three hours."

On same day, Mr. Lincoln telegraphed McClellan :

"What news from direction of Manassas Junction ? What generally ?"

On same day, McClellan telegraphed Halleck :

"Colonel Wagner, 2nd New York artillery, has just come in from the front. He reports infantry and cavalry force of rebels near Fairfax Court House. Reports rumors from various sources that Lee and Stuart, with large forces, are at Manassas. That the enemy, with 120,000 men intend advancing on the forts near Arlington and Chain Bridge, with a view of attacking Washington and Baltimore."

Even Burnside, down at Falmouth opposite Fredericksburg, had got badly scared, and at 6 P. M. on the 29th, telegraphed Halleck :

"A large body of the enemy reported opposite. I am preparing, and will hold the place until the last. The only fear I have, is a force coming from Manassas Junction."

## SECOND BATTLE OF MANASSAS.

Early in the day, on the 29th, the enemy opened a heavy fire of artillery on General Jackson's right, and it was vigorously responded to by our batteries on that flank, which were moved to the front for the purpose, when a fierce cannonade ensued that lasted for several hours. The enemy also pushed forward columns of infantry, on our left, into a body of woods that bordered on the rail-road grade all along the front of that portion occupied by our troops. There ensued a good deal of desultory fighting on that part of the line, in which the brigades of Thomas, Gregg, and Branch were principally engaged on our side, and Sigel's corps on the other side—the latter being finally driven from our front about noon.

In the meantime, about or a little before 11 A. M. the head of Longstreet's command, composed of Hood's two brigades, was seen advancing along the turnpike in my front, in line of battle, and the rest of the command soon came following close in the rear, when the whole commenced taking position on both sides of the turnpike, and to the rear of Jackson's right.

It was very apparent to me now, that the purpose for which I had been posted at the point I occupied had been completely sub-served by the interposition of Longstreet's forces between me and the force of the enemy reported to be advancing in that direction from Manassas, and that there was no further need for my presence there. I therefore determined to withdraw, without waiting for orders, and move to the left, where I was satisfied there was need for the two brigades under me. Hays's brigade was at once sent to the left to rejoin the division, and I proceeded to withdraw my two regiments from the front, which had been skirmishing, during the morning, with small bodies of the enemy that approach-ed them. As soon as they arrived, I moved the brigade to the woods in rear of the centre of our line on the rail-road grade, and reported to General Lawton. The brigade was here held in reserve for some time, having been joined on its left by the 8th Louisiana regiment of Hays's brigade, which had not been with its brigade during the morning.

In the afternoon, the enemy concentrated large bodies of infantry in the woods in front of Hill's position, and after a fierce artillery fire from numerous batteries on that flank, which was responded to with effect by Hill's batteries, the enemy's columns of infantry advanced against the position on the rail-road grade occupied by Hill's brigades, when a fierce and obstinate engagement, or rather series of engagements ensued, which lasted until very late in the afternoon. The troops most heavily engaged on this part of the line, were the brigades of Gregg, Thomas, and Field, but the other brigades of Hill's division went to their support and became also heavily engaged at different periods. The attacks of the enemy were persistent and repeated several times, new columns moving forward when others had been repulsed. General McGowan, who subsequently succeeded to the command of Gregg's brigade, and General Hill, report that there were seven separate and distinct attacks made at this point. In one of these attacks, a force of the enemy succeeded in penetrating a short uncovered interval between Gregg's right and Thomas's left, but was repulsed after a fierce struggle, in which at one time the fire of the opposing forces was delivered at ten paces. Hays's brigade, under Colonel Forno, went to the assistance of Hill's brigades soon after its arrival from the right and aided most gallantly in repulsing the enemy. Farther to the right, the enemy at another time succeeded in crossing the rail-road grade, when the brigades under Johnson and Stafford, respectively, moved forward to the attack, drove this force back and crossed the grade in pursuit. The brigade under Johnson captured a piece of artillery and the two then returned to their former positions.

About or a little after 4 P. M., the enemy made his seventh and last assault upon Gregg and Thomas with great fury, when, after a fierce struggle, their ammunition having become exhausted, they retired a short distance to the rear with the determination of using the bayonet. The enemy then crossed the rail-road grade, which at this point had a very deep cut, and occupied a skirt of woods adjoining it. Just at this time, one of General Hill's couriers came to me, with the information that the two brigades had been compelled to fall back from want of ammunition, and that the enemy was in possession of the cut, and requested me to go to the support of Gregg and Thomas and recover their position, at the same time informing me that the orders were not to cross the line of the grade, but to hold that line.

I immediately moved forward with my brigade and the 8th Louisiana, through an open field in front, and, being joined by the 13th Georgia on my right, which was preparing to move forward, passed the brigades of Gregg and Thomas, and attacked the enemy.

After a very brief struggle the enemy was driven across the cut, and the brigade, without having halted, followed in pursuit some two hundred yards beyond the grade, before I succeeded in stopping it. It was then moved back and occupied the position from which Gregg and Thomas had retired. The 13th Georgia on my right and the 8th Louisiana on my left, had crossed at the same time with my brigade. After our return, the enemy opened a furious fire from the front with cannister, but made no further advance with infantry.

This was the last attack on Jackson's line on the 29th, and the enemy had been defeated and foiled in all of his attacks. His troops engaged in these assaults in the afternoon, were the corps of Heintzelman and Reno, supported by Reynolds's division on their left—Sigel's corps had been so badly worsted in the forenoon that it was not able to unite in these attacks.

General Lee had ordered Longstreet to attack the enemy's left, on his arrival on the field about noon, but the latter, according to his own statements of recent date, had insisted on taking time to reconnoitre.

Some of his batteries, however, were placed in position, and opened on the enemy, who withdrew from his immediate front. Hood's brigades then took position across the Warrenton turnpike, west of Groveton, and were supported by Evans's brigade. Wilcox, with three brigades under him, took position on the north of the turnpike, in rear of Hood's left, and Kemper, with three other brigades, took position on the south of the turnpike, in rear of Hood's right, while D. R. Jones, with three other brigades, was posted on the Manassas Gap rail-road, to the right of Kemper, and in echelon with respect to him. A number of Longstreet's batteries were now posted on a commanding position between General Jackson's right and Longstreet's line, and engaged in the pending artillery duel with those of the enemy. The advance of the enemy on the right from the direction of Manassas, which was made by Porter's corps, having been reported, Wilcox's brigades were sent to re-inforce Jones, but the enemy retired after firing a few shots, and Wilcox returned to his former position. Stuart, who confronted Porter's corps with his cavalry, on the road from Manassas to Gainesville, had amused himself by having brush dragged up and down the road from the direction of Gainesville, to raise a dust, occasionally varying the amusement by firing a shot or two from his artillery in the direction of the enemy. Fitz Lee returned in the afternoon from his raid on the enemy's communications in the direction of Alexandria, and took position on our left near Sudley Mills, to protect the trains, which had been endangered during the day.

About sunset, General Longstreet ordered Hood to advance with his two brigades, supported by Evans's, along the turnpike and attack the enemy, but before Hood moved he was himself attacked by a column of the enemy which was moving along the turnpike in the direction of Gainesville.

McDowell's corps, which had been with Porter's on the road from Manassas to Gainesville, had moved to the right and taken position on Pope's left, and, about sunset, Pope ordered McDowell to push out on the turnpike towards Gainesville and cut off Jackson's retreat, under the hallucination that the latter had been de-

feated   King's division, being in the advance, encountered Hood
just as he was about to move forward, and a sharp action ensued,
the enemy being driven back and pursued for some distance until
the darkness compelled Hood to halt.   At 12 o'clock at night he
returned to his former position, and thus ended the fighting on the
29th, our troops remaining masters of the field on every part of it.

It is rather amusing to read some of Pope's statements about the
fighting on this day.   In his report, he says :

"Sigel attacked the enemy about daylight on the morning of the
29th, a mile or two east of Groveton, where he was soon joined by
the divisions of Kearney and Hooker.   Jackson fell back several
miles, but was so closely pressed by these forces that he was compelled to make a stand, and to make the best defence possible."

Speaking of the attack by Heintzelman and Reno in the afternoon, he says :

"The attack was made with great gallantry, and the whole of
the left of the enemy was doubled back towards his centre, and
our own forces, after a sharp conflict of an hour and half, occupied
the field of battle, with the dead and wounded of the enemy in our
hands."

At 5 A. M., on the 30th, he telegraphed Halleck in regard to
the battle of the day before :

"We have lost not less than eight thousand men killed and
wounded : but from the appearance of the field the enemy lost at
least two to one."

General Jackson's force must have been wiped out, then.

In the same dispatch he further says :

"The news just reaches me from the front that the enemy is retiring towards the mountains : I go forward at once to see.   We
have made great captures, but I am not able yet to form an idea
of their extent."

He had certainly caught a Tartar.

In his report, he says :

"Every indication, during the night of the 29th, and up to 10
o'clock on the morning of the 30th, pointed to the retreat of the
enemy from our front.   Paroled prisoners of our own, taken on
the evening of the 29th, and who came into our lines on the morning of the 30th, reported the enemy retreating during the whole

night in the direction of and along the Warrenton turnpike; Generals McDowell and Heintzelman, who reconnoitred the positions held by the enemy's left on the evening of the 29th, confirming this statement."

Why were *we* parolling prisoners? The most remarkable thing, however, connected with the battle of the 29th, is, perhaps, the fact that one of Pope's corps commanders, General Porter, was court-martialed and cashiered, for not marching over Longstreet's whole command, and cutting off Jackson's retreat, after the latter had defeated and repulsed three corps of Pope's army that largely more than doubled Porter's entire force.

On the morning of the 30th, our troops occupied the positions they held at the close of the battle the day before, with some slight shifting of the brigades on the rail-road grade, not necessary to mention. There was some heavy skirmishing in the forenoon along Jackson's line on the rail-road grade, especially on the left, but there was no assault at that time, the enemy being kept at bay. There was also some artillery firing on the right, which continued until the afternoon.

At noon Pope issued the following order to his troops:

"August 30th, 1862, 12 M.

"The following forces will be immediately thrown forward in pursuit of the enemy, and press him vigorously during the whole day. Major-General McDowell is assigned to the command of the pursuit.

Major-General Porter's corps will push forward on the Warrenton turnpike, followed by the divisions of Brigadier-Generals King and Reynolds.

The division of Brigadier-General Ricketts will pursue the Haymarket road, followed by the corps of Major-General Heintzelman; the necessary cavalry will be assigned to these columns by Major-General McDowell, to whom regular and frequent reports will be made. The general head-quarters will be somewhere on the Warrenton turnpike."

In the afternoon, there was a slight change in the programme, and Porter's corps supported by King's division advanced against Jackson's right and Heintzelman's and Reno's corps supported, for a time by Ricketts's division, advanced against our left. The assaults began about 3 P. M., and were very fierce and determined, especially on the right where Jackson's division was posted but, were met with equal determination.

There were at least three assaults on Jackson's division, following each other in succession, which were repulsed, some of the men of the brigades commanded by Stafford and Johnson, using stones when their ammunition was exhausted. Longstreet's batteries, by a well directed fire from the right on the flank of the attacking columns, contributed largely to their repulse. The assaults on the left were also fierce, but were successfully resisted by the brigades of Archer and Thomas, supported by those of Pender and Fields. There was no serious attack on the centre occupied by Ewell's division, but as one of the attacking columns was retiring from the right past our front, one or two heavy volleys were poured into it, and three of my regiments that were on the railroad grade, suddenly dashed across it, in pursuit, without orders, but were soon brought back.

R. H. Anderson's division had arrived during the forenoon, and joined Longstreet's command ; and finally, about 4 P. M., after the last attack on Jackson's right had been repulsed, Longstreet ordered his infantry to attack the enemy's left, and his troops moved forward, with Hood in the lead closely followed by Evans. They were rapidly supported by Anderson's division, and the brigades under Kemper, D. R. Jones, and Wilcox. The enemy was assailed with great vigor, and he was steadily driven before Longstreet's advancing lines, from successive positions which he occupied, though at some points the assaults were stubbornly resisted for a time. General Jackson's command had also advanced at the same time in pursuit of the troops that had been repulsed, and some of Hill's brigades encountered and engaged a part of the retreating forces on the left, which they pursued to Bull Run, capturing a number of pieces of artillery. Jackson's and Ewell's divisions did did not become engaged with the enemy in the pursuit. Longstreet's command continued to press the enemy on the right until his whole army was driven across Bull Run, when darkness put an end to the pursuit. This command captured several batteries of artillery.

Near the close of the battle on this day, General Robertson, with a portion of his cavalry, attacked and routed a body of the enemy's cavalry on the extreme right.

At the close of the battle we were masters of the entire field; and, in the series of engagements on the plains of Manassas, we had captured more than 7,000 prisoners, besides 2,000 wounded left on our hands, thirty pieces of artillery, upwards of twenty thousand stand of small arms, a number of regimental colors, and a considerable amount of stores. Our own loss in killed and wounded was 7,224, including a number of valuable officers, some of them of high rank.

Pope's army retired to Centreville that night, where it was re-inforced by Sumner's and Franklin's corps of McClellan's army.

In his report, after having previously stated that: "Every indication during the night of the 29th, and up to 10 o'clock on the morning of the 30th, pointed to the retreat of the enemy from our front;" he says, two pages further on:

"During the whole night of the 29th, and the morning of the 30th, the advance of the main army, under Lee, was arriving on the field to re-inforce Jackson, so that by 12 or 1 o'clock in the day we were confronted by forces greatly superior to our own; and these forces were being every moment largely increased by fresh arrivals of the enemy from the direction of Thoroughfare Gap."

The Confederate soldier, though ragged, nearly barefooted, and often hungry, had a wonderful faculty of multiplying himself on the field of battle, so as to present the appearance of "overwhelming numbers" to a frightened enemy.

On the night of the 30th, at 9.45 P. M., Pope telegraphed Halleck:

"We have had a terrific battle again to-day. The enemy, largely re-inforced, assaulted our position early to-day. We held our ground firmly until 6 o'clock P. M. when the enemy massing very heavy forces on our left, forced back that wing about half a mile. At dark we held that position. Under all circumstances—both horses and men having been two days without food, and the enemy greatly outnumbering us—I thought it best to move back to this place at dark. The movement has been made in perfect order and without loss. The troops are in good heart, and marched off the field without the least hurry or confusion. Their conduct was very fine. The battle was most furious for hours without cessation, and the losses on both sides very heavy. The enemy is badly whipped, and we shall do well enough. Do not be uneasy. We will hold our own here."

At 11 A. M. next day, Halleck telegraphed Pope:

"My Dear General: You have done nobly. Don't yield another inch if you can avoid it. All reserves are being sent forward."

Before this, at 10.45 A. M., Pope had telegraphed Halleck:

"Our troops are all here, and in position, though much used up and worn out. I think perhaps it would have been greatly better if Sumner and Franklin had been here three or four days ago; but you may rely upon our giving them as desperate a fight as I can force our men to stand up to. I should like to know whether you feel secure about Washington, should this army be destroyed. I shall fight it as long as a man will stand up to the work."

What a wonderful collapse from the tone of his salutatory address to his troops is here exhibited. He had by this time learned a thing or two; but his mind seems to have become as confused by this newly acquired knowledge as Banks's.

On the 31st, Longstreet, with his command including Anderson's division, was left on the battlefield to engage the attention of the enemy, and cover the burial of the dead and the removal of the wounded, while General Jackson moved his command across Bull Run at and below Sudley Ford, for the purpose of turning the enemy's right and intercepting his retreat. Moving to the left over country roads, we reached the Little River turnpike, leading from Aldie past Germantown and Fairfax C. H. to Alexandria, late in the afternoon; and after moving on that road for a short distance we bivouacked for the night. On the next morning (1st of September) the march was resumed, Hill's division being in the advance. At Ox Hill, near Chantilly, a large force of the enemy was encountered, in the afternoon, which had been moved out in that direction to cover Pope's retreat along the turnpike from Centreville to Fairfax C. H. He had now ascertained that it was very necessary to look out for his line of retreat, as well as his base of supplies. Hill at once attacked the enemy with a part of his division, and Ewell's division also moved up and became engaged.

There was a sharp conflict which lasted until near night, in which the elements took part with a severe thunder-storm; and two of the Federal Generals, Kearney and Stevens, were killed. At the close of the fight, we held possession of the field, and the enemy retired during the night. The troops encountered on this occasion belonged to McDowell's and Reno's corps, and Kearney's division, there being also some troops newly arrived from Alexandria and Washington, of which Hooker had command. Longstreet's command came up at night after the action had closed.

The next morning it was discovered that Pope had now learned the art of retreating so well, that it was impracticable to intercept him, and he was permitted to take refuge in the fortifications of Washington, without further molestation.

Thus ended the campaign of August, 1862.

In a few days Pope was relieved from his command, and sent to the Northwest to look after the Indians in that quarter, so that he never again had the opportunity to look at the backs or faces of the "rebels."

Sitting Bull had not then made his appearance on the theatre of war, or we might never more have heard of Major General John Pope.

## RESUME OF THE CAMPAIGN.

It is impossible at this day to give the exact strength of the forces engaged on our side in this campaign, from the Rapidan to Ox Hill, as the returns, if regularly made, have been lost or destroyed. I have given the estimate of General Jackson's strength at the battle of Cedar Run, and in the subsequent campaign it could not have exceeded that estimate—that is, about 20,000 officers and men for duty, in his infantry and artillery. His effective strength, that is, enlisted men for duty who bear arms, was probably about 18,500. General Longstreet's command consisted of his own division of six brigades, divided into two sub-divisions of three brigades each, D. R. Jones's division of three brigades, Hood's division of two brigades, and Evans's brigade.

On the 20th of July, according to the official returns as given by Colonel Walter H. Taylor, in the work I have referred to, the strength of that command, with the exception of Drayton's brigade which had been added to Jones's division, and Evans's brigade, both of which arrived from the South after the 20th of July, was as follows :

|  | OFFICERS. | ENLISTED MEN. |
|---|---|---|
| Longstreet's division, | 557 | 7,929 |
| D. R. Jones's division, | 213 | 3,500 |
| Hood's [Whiting's] division, | 252 | 3,600 |
| Total, | 1,022 | 15,029 |

General Evans, in his report, says that his brigade had an aggregate for duty, on the 30th of July, of 1,862, which was subsequently increased to 2,200 by the addition of the 23rd South Carolina regiment. There is no return of the strength of Drayton's brigade, but Colonel Taylor, on the authority of the Adjutant General of the brigade, puts the aggregate for duty of that brigade and Evans's at 4,600,* of which at least 350 must have been officers. Longstreet's strength, therefore, before the arrival of Anderson's division, was about 1,372 officers and 19,279 enlisted men, or an aggregate of 20,651. Anderson's division, according to the return of July 20th, was 357 officers and 5,760 enlisted men for duty, which would give Longstreet, with Anderson's division added to his command, 1,729 officers and 25,039 enlisted men, or an aggregate of 26,768 for duty. Colonel Taylor estimates the artillery at 2,500 and the cavalry at the same number, which would give an aggregate of the entire force of 51,768, and an effective force of less than 49,000, without making any deduction for losses.

The divisions of D. H. Hill and McLaws, two brigades under J. G. Walker, and Hampton's brigade of cavalry,† which had been left near Richmond, and were ordered up after the entire evacuation of Harrison's Landing, did not join us until after the fight at Ox Hill, and Pope had taken refuge under the fortifications of Washington.

---

*NOTE.—This must be an over-estimate, as Drayton's brigade had only three regiments and a batallion. The estimate would give that brigade 2,400, or an average of 600 for the three regiments and one batallion. Rather too much for Confederate regiments at that day. The brigade was so small after Sharpsburg, though its losses had not been severe in the campaign, that the regiments and batallion of which it was composed were distributed among other brigades.

†NOTE.—General Hampton has informed me that his brigade was up by the 1st of September; but it had not arrived in time to take part in any of the previous actions, and the other commands, being infantry, did not arrive until the 2nd.

General McClellan, in his official report, shows that, by the 1st of March 1862, he had organized an army of 193,142 men for duty, who were in and about Washington, or within easy reach thereof. He had carried largely more than 100,000 of that army to the Peninsula, leaving the rest to defend the Federal Capital. Fremont had brought his corps, which was largely from Missouri and the West, to the Valley in the month of May, and his corps numbered 15,000 or 20,000. Burnside, in July, had brought about 13,000 men from North Carolina to the vicinity of Fredericksburg, 8,000 of which had been sent to Pope on the 14th of August. The whole of McClellan's army, which he had at Harrison's Landing, except one division of Keys's corps, had been sent to Pope, though Sumner's and Franklin's corps did not reach him until the 31st of August, and Couch's division of Keys's corps joined him at Fairfax C. H. on the 1st of September, the day of the fight at Ox Hill. Moreover, Cox had arrived from the Kanawha Valley with 7,000 men. It was then what was left of some 220,000 or 230,000 men, that General Lee's army of about 50,000 men had forced to take refuge in the defences of Washington to escape destruction.*

What had become of the balance?

It may be said that a great many had been lost in the previous campaigns, in the Valley and around Richmond. But McClellan's official return of the 20th of July shows more than 90,000 men for duty, exclusive of Dix's corps at Fortress Monroe. Pope acknowledges that he had 43,000 in the beginning, after striking off 6,400 men for Banks's corps from his own official return, and he had been joined by 8,000 men under Reno and 3,500 under Piatt. Here then were at least 140,000, after making an allowance for Keys's absent division, and not counting Cox's 7,000, the balance of Sturgis's command, or the new troops mentioned by Halleck and Pope. But Pope says his men and horses were much used up and worn out, and without food. Well, I suppose the poor "rebels" were living in clover all this time. There is one advantage we

---

*NOTE.—The army of General Lee in the campaign against McClellan did not exceed 80,000 officers and men, as I have demonstrated on another occasion. The only re-inforcements he received from the South, or any other quarter, after that campaign and previous to the campaign against Pope, consisted of the brigades of Evans and Drayton, and perhaps two Alabama regiments. Some of the troops engaged in the "Seven Days Battles," besides the divisions of D. H. Hill, McLaws, and J. G. Walker, were left near Richmond, and did not participate at all in the campaign against Pope, or that into Maryland.

had over Pope very certainly—we had nothing for him to capture, and we got into his supply train at Manassas; but even that did not last very long. On the night of the 1st of September, at Ox Hill, I made my dinner and my supper on two ears of green corn, which I roasted by the fire while sitting on the damp ground; and on the next day, while passing through my brigade, I saw the rations being issued to my men, and they consisted exclusively of cold boiled fresh beef, without salt or bread. I helped myself to a small chunk, which I munched to still the cravings of hunger. There were few, if any, in our army, from the highest to the lowest, any better off than I was.

I will give you one more and the last quotation from Pope's official report. He had said in his address to his troops: "I have come to you from the West, where we have always seen the backs of our enemies—from an army whose business it has been to seek the adversary and beat him when found, whose policy has been attack and not defence;" and in a dispatch to Kearney at 9 P. M. on the 27th: "Jackson, A. P. Hill, and Ewell are in front of us. Hooker has had a severe fight with them to-day. McDowell marches upon Manassas Junction from Gainesville to-morrow at day-break. Reno upon the same place at the same hour. I want you here at day-dawn, if possible, and we will bag the whole crowd." Yet he has the following doleful reflections in the concluding part of his official report:

"To confront, with a small army, vastly superior forces: to fight battles without hope of victory, but only to gain time, and to embarrass and delay the forward movement of the enemy, is of all duties, the most hazardous and the most difficult that can be imposed upon any General or any army. While such operations require the highest courage and endurance on the part of the troops, they are, perhaps, unlikely to be understood or appreciated, and the results, however successful, have little in them to attract popular attention and applause. At no time could I have hoped to fight a successful battle with the immensely superior force of the enemy which confronted me, and which was able at any time to out-flank me and bear my small army to the dust."

"O, what a fall was there, my countrymen!"

The result of this campaign was that Virginia was cleared of the invading army, except at Fortress Monroe and its vicinity. Norfolk where the enemy's men-of-war and gun-boats enabled him to hold his position, the fortifications covering Washington on the South, and North-western Virginia, where traitors and renegades, under the protection of Federal bayonets, had established a bastard State Government. Even the Kanawha Valley had been cleared of the enemy, as the withdrawal of troops from that quarter, for the defence of Washington, had enabled Loring to penetrate into the Valley and drive the enemy from it.

There have been criticisms of the strategy employed by General Lee in sending Jackson to the rear of Pope, thus dividing his army and placing the smaller portion between two hostile forces of superior numbers. This is said by some to have been in violation of the established rules of war. Genius is trammelled by no arbitrary rules, but is able to burst the fetters which bind ordinary intellects. With vastly inferior forces and resources, if General Lee had conformed to the ordinary rules of war, he would, perhaps, have taken some defensive position and waited until the enemy had accumulated forces sufficient to overwhelm him, or retired before the enemy's superior numbers, thus giving up the whole country his troops were fighting for, and gradually losing his army by exhaustion and desertion. But he knew that it was necessary to make up for the deficiency in other respects by activity, energy, genius.

We are told that, when the young Napoleon made his first campaign in Italy, he startled the European Generals of the old school by his disregard of the recognized tactics and science of war, and they thought him wild and crazy, but he defeated his opponents nevertheless. And so some military critics, of the red tape order, may think General Lee committed a great blunder on this occasion, but it was a very successful blunder,

A General should be able to understand his opponent, as well as the instruments he himself employs.

General Lee thoroughly understood Pope, and he knew, and fully appreciated General Jackson. In a letter to General Porter, written in July, 1870, General Lee, in a very few plain words, expressed volumes—he said:

"I had no anxiety for Jackson at 2nd Manassas. I knew he could hold on till we came, and that we should be in position in time."

There was no man in all our armies who was so bold and daring in his strategy and his operations as General Lee, and the difficulty he labored under was to find agents to carry out the plans he designed. General Jackson was just the man he wanted. Whatever General Lee devised or suggested, General Jackson was ready to carry out promptly and without question or cavil as to its feasibility. The confidence they had in each other was mutual, and there was no man in all the South, whether in or out of the army, upon whom the loss of General Jackson fell so heavily as upon General Lee. In this campaign against Pope, General Jackson displayed greater ability and resources than on any other occasion, because the circumstances by which he was surrounded required such display; and he fully justified the confidence reposed in him by General Lee.

And now, my comrades, when called upon for a defence or justification of the cause in which you were enlisted, you can point proudly and confidently to the characters of the great leaders whom you followed—Lee and Jackson—for your complete vindication.

When the captive Israelites sat down by the rivers of Babylon and wept, the sacred psalmist put into their mouths the following language:

"If I forget thee, O, Jerusalem, let my right hand forget her cunning."

"If I do not remember thee, let my tongue cleave to the roof of my mouth; if I prefer not Jerusalem above my chief joy."

I trust that every faithful soldier of the Army of Northern Virginia is ready to exclaim with me:

"If ever I disown, repudiate, or apologize for, the cause for which Lee fought and Jackson died, let the lightnings of Heaven blast me, and the scorn of all good men and true women be my portion."

MAJ. GEN'L. I. R. TRIMBLE.

# THE THIRD ANNUAL BANQUET

—— OF THE ——

# Society of the Army and Navy

# OF THE CONFEDERATE STATES

IN THE STATE OF MARYLAND,

HELD AT

# THE CARROLLTON HOTEL,

*FEBRUARY 22, 1883.*

# The Society of the Army & Navy of the Confederate States

The Society of the Army and Navy of the Confederate States in the State of Maryland is the Maryland Division of the Association of the Army of Northern Virginia, formed at Richmond, Virginia, in 1870, of which the Division of Louisiana, at New Orleans is a strong and enthusiastic auxiliary.

The Society in Maryland was organized so as to embrace all Confederates, without regard to the branch or locality of service.

It has recently added a Beneficial Society to its machinery, and an awakening enthusiasm, and interest, has been aroused, which will largely increase its membership and consequent usefulness.

The Third Annual Banquet of the Society took place at the Carrollton Hotel, after the conclusion of General Early's address and was attended by a large and enthusiastic assemblage—about one hundred and seventy five gentlemen sat down to the entertainment.

It was presided over by General Bradley T. Johnson, the President, with General Early on his right, General Wade Hampton on his left, General Trimble, General Stuart, Lt. Col. J. R. Herbert, Captain Waddell, Colonel Herbert, late of the 8th Alabama, now Member of Congress from that State, Rev. W. M. Dame, Hon. J. F. C. Talbott, late private 2nd Maryland Cavalry, now Member of Congress from Maryland, Major H. Kyd Douglas, Colonel J. Lyle Clarke, Captain McHenry Howard and many other prominent Confederates from the State.

After an earnest discussion of the Bill of Fare, the President arose and called the meeting to order and read the Toasts.

# TOASTS.

## Our Infantry.

With hearts as light as their haversacks, but as true and steadfast as the barrels of their muskets, they fought hunger, hard-
ship and overwhelming numbers for four years; the simple recital of their deeds is their highest encomium.

RESPONDED TO BY

## Major Gen. J. R. Trimble,

TRIMBLE'S DIVISION, A. N. VA

## Our Cavalry.

First in the front, last in the rear. The Artillery rested sometimes; the Infantry rarely; the Cavalry, never.

RESPONDED TO BY

## Lt. Col. Clement Sulivane,

A. A. G. CUSTIS LEE'S DIVISION, A. N. VA.

## Our Artillery.

Though occasionally their room was better than their company,
by reason of the marked attention which they attracted from
the enemy, as a rule they were very welcome—except
to the people opposite.

RESPONDED TO BY

## Col. David G. McIntosh,

McINTOSH'S BATTALION ARTILLERY, A. N. VA.

## Our Navy.

Ready for service wherever duty called; in the batteries at Acquia
Creek, or in the breast-works at Petersburg; from Hampton
Roads to Mobile Bay, in the hour of disaster not less than
in the day of victory; they added lustre to the cause
they loved; they made all seas acquainted with
our flag; they bore it farthest and they
furled it last.

RESPONDED TO BY

## Capt. James J. Waddell,

C. S. S. S. SHENANDOAH.

# OUR DEAD.

RESPONDED TO BY

## Rev. W. M. Dame,

PRIVATE 1ST RICHMOND HOWITZERS, A. N. VA.
Mr. Dame made a telling speech, but it was not reported.

# "OUR INFANTRY."

*"With hearts as light as their haversacks, but as true and steadfast as the barrels of their muskets, they fought hunger, hardships and overwhelming numbers for four years; the simple recital of their deeds is their highest encomium."*

MR. PRESIDENT, COMRADES AND FRIENDS.

I was at a loss at first, to understand why the Committee selected me—a mounted officer—to speak for the Infantry. For *two* out of four years of the war, I had but one foot I could call my own; the other being in the hands of the manufacturers. But I discovered the delicate irony intended to cover my defect; that being literally *a foot* soldier it was appropriate that I should speak for the Infantry.

Our Infantry! What a theme for the orator, the historian and the poet! No one has done nor for a long time can do it justice.

From the 19th of April, 1861, when volunteers began singly and in squads to cross that River, which only divides, but does not *separate* Maryland from grand, glorious Old Virginia; and to hasten from the Ranches of Texas; the glades of Louisiana; the cotton fields of Mississippi and Alabama, of Georgia, of Florida, and South Carolina, and from the dark mountains and sombre pines of the "Old North State;" to the day they laid down their arms under the apple tree at Appomattox; the exploits of the Infantry surpassed in heroism and endurance those of any recorded in the history of modern warfare.

What marching and fighting! What privations in food and clothing! What sublime endurance in unprotected camps and in long marches in drenching rains, in winter's cold and in summer's heat! What enthusiasm exhibited as engagements with the enemy approached and with what intrepid valor in the shock of conflict! These deeds have given the Infantry of the South, a name not inferior to any of modern times, and that will live in history and verse, as long as chivalric deeds shall excite the admiration of mankind.

No voice nor pen can do justice to the wonderful exploits of the Southern Soldier; to brave, patient, indomitable "Johnny Reb."

I know that I am no orator, but why should I not *try* to extol his prowess? We marched together; we fought together; we starved together. That superb Brigade (the 7th) composed of the 21st Georgia, 21st North Carolina, 15th Alabama and 16th Mississippi, with that unmatched battery of the "boy" Latimer— the peer of any in the service— *all* by their splendid fighting, made me a Major General. I therefore owe them something.

From the day I first led them into battle in Jackson's glorious campaign and only left them when wounded at 2d Manasses; it was their splendid behavior there, and in after battles, which promoted from their officers, 7 *Brigadiers* and 6 *Major Generals*. Yes my comrades; but it was not the 7th Brigade alone which conferred such honors. It was the *men* of the Brigades *everywhere;* who by their courage and "dash" made all our commanders in the Army of Northern Virginia and in the South and West, save Lee and Jackson. They were Nature's Heroes. They were made by the hand of the Great Father above, who commands the Armies in Heaven and on Earth.

Yes, although able chieftains planned campaigns and directed skillful manœuvres in the field, it was "Johnny Reb" *who won the battles, and yet was never promoted.* I think I will attempt this evening to do him tardy justice, and appoint him, over all grades, to the rank of "*General Johnny Reb.*" He was as great as any of our chieftains; and if there was any one *greater* than he, it was "Johnny Reb's" wife. Did not she enlist nearly all our soldiers, *without paying one dollar of "bounty,"* and send them to the field to join hands and hearts with the sons of glorious Old Virginia? And if they had not "marched pretty quick," there would have been fought more domestic "scrimmages" "away down South in Dixie," than Lee and Jackson fought in Virginia. Well! they did "obey orders," and come. And who of us here, my comrades, would not have done the same, and freely shed the last drop of his blood for woman's protection and a mother's approving smile. **Yes!** they came with high resolve to defend a cause which they believed to be right. How many of them came too, to fill "unnamed" graves?

But what a picture, in general, did they present when first among us in Richmond? No gay uniforms; no martial step; no florid faces; no erect forms; true some from cities did come "bedecked in all the panoply of war." Who that had seen the gaudy splendor of "trained armies," could suppose that these half bent, lounging forms would ever make good soldiers. I confess I had my doubts and only hoped for success in their proverbial bravery and their sure skill with the musket. "Johnny" could shoot deer and squirrels at home with the rifle, then why could he not hit a Federal Soldier?

How were we all mistaken in their fighting and marching qualities, and in their almost sublime patience under bitter hardships of all kinds?

In after days when they won battles, well might Swinton, a Northern historian, call them *"that incomparable* Infantry with bright muskets and ragged jackets."

Well! so "our Johnny Rebs" were drilled in haste and formed into Regiments and Brigades, the greater number armed with old flint-lock muskets, converted into percussion locks; but in every battle he picked up better arms, dropped in a hurry, by Yankee "braves."

The Brigades of the Army were the proper nucleus of its organization and strength; of its "Esprit de Corps"; its reliance in the stern conflict and for the dashing charges that won the day.

Brigades were handled with more facility and expedition on the march and in the battle. The men knew well their Brigade commanders who were ever present with them, to share the toils and exposures of the service, as well as the perils of battle. And if "Johnny" had faith in his Brigadier; could hear his voice, or see his form; things always "went right."

I have said the men of Brigades made all our Generals. They also did some discourteous things in *another way*. They *cashiered* in a very reckless manner; without intending to hurt their feelings, some six or seven commanding Generals on the *Federal* side, and made "Old Joe Hooker" and others of that sort "get out of the way."

When was it that some Brigade was not called on to repel an advance? or by a charge to end a battle? and where was it that with such officers as Taylor, Gordon, Winder, Hoke, Wilcox, Lane, Early, Hampton, Johnson and Herbert, and a score of others like them; that the Infantry ever failed to win the day? How was it at the *first* and *second* Manassas? How in Jackson's Valley Campaign? How at Coal Harbor? How at Fredericksburg? How at Chancellorsville? And how in that indomitable struggle in the wilderness and at Spottsylvania Court House against odds of 3 to 1? How *everywhere* in a charge, save at Malvern Hill and Gettysburg, where *impossibilities* were attempted, but where the "boys" could show how they scorned death if they could not conquer? And how was it my comrades, when that Brigade cheer "that appalling rebel yell" as Yankees called it—once heard, never forgotten—which for four years of bloody strife sent back its echos to every battlefield in "Old Virginia?"

There is no need to answer these questions. Time and just history have answered them all; and told that this triumphant cheer was everywhere the harbinger of victory; and when heard afar amid the discords of battle, "we-uns" knew that "you-uns" had finished the work in hand.

## THE VALLEY CAMPAIGN.

Some of us Marylanders were in that brilliant campaign of Jackson, and we knew that some "pretty tall" marching as well as fighting was done there. It was there that the Southern Soldier, unused at home to walking any distance, or "toating" any burden, (always choosing to saddle his horse for a long ride of *half a mile* to visit a neighbor,) first exhibited his wonderful powers of endurance and resolution. Such marching qualities introduced that new feature in the organization of an army.—The Foot Cavalry.

## DISTANCE MARCHED BY JACKSON.

On a fair computation of the distances marched from the battle of Kearnstown to McDowell and thence back and forth to the end of the campaign at Port Republic; over 500 *miles* were made in 90 *days*, inclusive of time given to battles and reorganization of forces at Conrad's store. Deducting for battles and imperative halts, these troops marched an average of 12 miles a day, many days 30 miles in spite of heat, rains and bad roads.

In this period they fought *five* decisive battles, winning all but one, (and that not a defeat) against adversaries *all around them,* numbering in the aggregate *four men* to Jackson's one. When escaping from the snares that beset his path and reaching Strasburg on the evening of May 31st; McDowell on his left, was near Front Royal with 30,000 men, only 12 miles from Strasburg. Fremont was at Wardensville on his right, 20 miles from Strasburg; with 14,600 men—both together numbering near 45,000 men; while Banks, south of the Potomac and but 50 miles from Strasburg, had 14,000 men. (but Jackson never took much account of Banks, save for his commissary stores.) Thus making four times the force of Jackson's 15,000. And yet the Federal forces missed their prey. Jackson was out of their toils and the "Foot Cavalry" did it. Winder had marched over 50 miles in 30 hours. Is it surprising that Lincoln was scared and that the World gazed in wonder? Or that another *small* batch of 100,000 men was called for to defend Washington? Such marching and fighting has no example in military history since the conquest of Gaul by Cæsar.

The only occasions when our Infantry could not surpass the Federals in marching, were those when the latter were "going to the rear." I have often wondered at the surprising "nack" they had in getting away from us. I suppose it was because they went "in light marching order," without knapsack, musket or overcoat.

### "STAYING."

Of all the soldier-like qualities of "Johnny Reb," the most conspicuous was what is known on "the turf," as the "staying" quality, as well illustrated in the "*Old* North State," as in any other. If hungry, he *stayed* hungry with a patience beyond belief. If eating, by *chance*, a good supper; he *stayed* at it a long time. If ordered to march, he *stayed* struggling on the best he could. If ordered to hold a position, he *stayed* there. If ordered to a charge, he *stayed* "agoing" until the enemy were out of sight. It is true "Johnny did sometimes *stay behind*—not to "skulk,"—but to drag his weary body along with all the strength left in him. And when a fight was on hand, he happened *somehow* to be there.

It was General Lee's profound confidence in the steady valor and "staying" quality of his troops that made him boldly encounter on all occasions, the great odds against him. As at Fredericksburg

and Chancellorsville, two to one. In the Wilderness, three to
one. General Grant had 145,000 men, Lee but 43,000 the first
day, (and at no time after, more than 54,000 men)—and these,
fighting the *first* day for the most part in Brigades against over-
welming odds: at one time, against odds of ten to one. Be it
always *remembered* that from the beginning of that fierce struggle
in the Wilderness to the end of the contest at Coal Harbor—that
is, from the 5th of May to the 3d of June.—General Grant's losses
in killed and wounded were more in numbers, than General Lee's
entire Army, causing General Grant to send on the 7th of May
for reinforcements, at Washington and from other points.*

For the two first years of the War, victory perched on the banners of the Southern Army. Everywhere in Virginia, at Bull Run
and Manassas; in Jackson's Valley Campaign against Banks, at
McDowell, Winchester, Cross Keys and Port Republic; in the
seven days around Richmond—at Gaines' Mill, Coal Harbor,
Savage Station, Fraser's Farm, and Malvern Hill. Five battles
in 7 days. Then again, at Slaughter's Mountain, and at second
Manassas where there were 3 days fighting and 3 victories. Then
at Fredericksburg and at Chancellorsville. Yes my comrades,
continuous victories for two years.

Well appointed Federal Armies failed in five attempts to march
on Richmond and were driven out of Virginia by Confederate
forces, never more than one-half of those opposed to them, and
often less than one-third; and all the time with inferior arms,
clothing and equipments; and vastly inferior Commissary and
Quarter Master's and medical stores, hospital supplies, &c., &c.

*General Grant entered the "Wilderness" with 145,000 men of all arms.
I have the authority of Colonel Charles Marshall, for stating that General
Lee's force when he left Mine Run was not over 43,000 men. With part of
Ewell's corps, he fiercely assailed the Federal advance on the 5th May and
drove back parts of *three* corps.
On the 7th at noon, Longstreet arrived with 11,000 men, and drove back the
Federal right, with great slaughter. Lee's aggregate then numbered 54,000
men. The contest was fiercely waged, daily, until the 13th, when Grant's forces
were everywhere repulsed. He then called for reinforcements from Washington; and did not resume the offensive until the 18th. Breckenridge and
Hoke joined Lee with 12,000 men, just before the bloody contest at Coal
Harbor, by which time Grant had received re-inforcements amounting to 45,000
men, making his aggregate forces, that crossed the Rappahannock 190,000 men.
General Lee's aggregate, inclusive of Breckenridge and Hoke did not exceed
66,000 It is a significant fact, that, notwithstanding the ample appliances of
the Federal army, their dead, in these battles, were left unburied and the
wounded left on the field uncared for.

It is well known that ample and regular supplies of food and clothing contribute greatly to the good discipline, high spirits and *morale* of an army—the best assurance of victories. Their deficiency; to its discontent, depression of spirits, and that absence of enthusiasm, which is often-times the precursor of defeat.

Now it is beyond dispute that no armies since the beginning of this century were so *completely* equipped as were those of the Federal Government; while it is equally indisputable that those of the South were as signally deficient in all these essential requisites. Hence to great inferiority of numbers might be added the supposed disheartening influence of scanty and irregular supplies of all kinds, to impair the efficiency of the Southern Soldier. But in such a *cause* and with such *leaders*, these privations, but added to their strength; and it was found to be true of the Southern Infantry, as of Soldiers in all armies that "poverty, privation and want are the school of the good soldier." If these could make soldiers, then Lee's army was the best *training school* the world has ever known.

To truly describe the general condition of our men seems now like gross exaggeration. In my brigade when marching on Winchester, May 24th, twenty-five per cent. of the men were *bare footed* and the rest with shoes, only in name. It was a rare thing to see a soldier with overcoat, or blanket, or knapsack. Next day however, General Banks's stores in Winchester supplied them with all these most needed wants as well as abundant rations.

I once heard of a man in the West, who had invented a boat to run in very low water, to keep open the navigation of the Ohio in summer months. It would run in *two* feet, *one* foot, *six inches* of water; in fact, if no water could be found, he said it would run where the ground was *only a little moist*.

I think "Johnny Reb's" appetite much resembles the wonderful performance of that western boat. It would carry him along with only a little bacon grease, or even with the *smell* of Banks's commissary stores—Hams all cooked ready for us.

If any one doubts the superiority of the Southern Soldier, let him suppose the relative numbers in battles *reversed*, and then ask what would have been the result?

Would the ablest and boldest of the Federal Generals have been rash enough to hurl 50,000 of their best men against Lee in command of 100,000 Southern Infantry ? If they had done so, who can doubt what the result would have been ?

It was often said by Yankee Soldiers in *social converse* on the picket line, "Oh! if we had such generals as Lee and Jackson, we could whip you." Does not this idea admit the superiority of our soldiers and generals as fully as any one can expect.*

## DESERTION.

I would like, if time permitted, to say a word about desertions.

"Johnny" did not understand the meaning of "desertion," as defined by "the Articles of War." He probably never taxed himself with reading such "heavy stuff", and I don't think they were ever read to him on "parade inspection."

He thought it no harm to go home after a hard campaign, tell his story of battles, see "the old folks at home" and return in time for another fight.

I well remember, after our battles around Richmond, when we were recuperating our exhausted strength at Liberty Mills; that the Colonel of the 21st North Carolina regiment came to my tent one morning and reported that *forty* men, the night before, had left his command. I said "Colonel this is a very serious matter and must be promptly attended to; can't these men be pursued and arrested ? He "thought they could not be, until they reached their homes, but the effect of arresting them, and of trying them

---

*NOTE.—The Southern Soldier was full of expedients for bettering his condition; by mitigating the pangs of hunger; by supplying deficiency in clothing, and by restoring the frequently exhausted ammunition. His ingenuity invented "Stone Soap" and raw hide shoes; and the appropriation of the arms, ammunition, knapsacks, &c., of dead or defeated enemies, often restored his exhausted supplies of these articles. His confidence, coolness and bravery never forsook him on the march, or in the conflict; and his propensity for fun and jest broke out in the midst of dangers in the heat of battle. Said a Soldier to his comrade, in a lull of battle in the "Wilderness": "Taint no use to shoot these Yankees, if you kill ten of em, twenty steps into their places— but the dead 'uns' act fair, they leave us their loaded muskets." "Come out of these boots, my friend," as a Soldier said when taking that article from a dead enemy.

It is a well authenticated fact, that in the severe and bloody conflict in the *Wilderness*, against numbers, which would have been overwhelming on open ground, our men ingeniously supplemented their deficiency of numbers, by collecting on many occasions, arms-full of muskets and cartridge boxes from dead or defeated enemies, carrying them to the rear; ready for the next onslaught of Grant's forces. Saying "Its a pity to waste so much fine ammunition, and I reckon *thar* is no orders *agin* shooting Yankees with their own guns. It saves taking prisoners."

and sentencing them to be shot would have a bad effect and deter effectually, other citizens from that State from entering the Army." "But Colonel that matter is not for us to consider; desertion in this wholesale way must be stopped." "But," he rejoined, "General these men are not really deserters, they will come back again in two weeks or so, if let alone; and if I am not much mistaken, will bring more men with them." I was so much impressed by what he said, that I concluded to try the experiment and say no more about it. Before the expiration of the three weeks, the Colonel appeared one morning with a cheerful face, and said—"Well General my *deserters* have all come back." "Forty of them." I replied, "this is good news." "Yes" he said, "but the best news is, that they have brought back with them *thirty one* new recruits."

This presented certainly, a novel condition of things, and might well call for some modification of the "Articles of War" in relation to "desertion."

In calling up these men, I delivered, with as much gravity as I could assume, a lecture on the evil of desertion, which might, as practiced by them, disband the whole army, at a crisis in military movements. I then dismissed them with what I thought the keenest reproach I could utter, viz: "How would you have felt, men, if we had fought a battle when you were away?" One of them replied without any tears in his eye too, "Oh! we knew that 'Old Stonewall' had to rest his men; but General if a battle had come off, we would have been *thar* somehow."

Knowing the temper, and child-like simplicity, yet the true loyalty of the Southern Soldier; and that they all, in the beginning, had been volunteers; I was always opposed to shooting, what were called "deserters."

If any of these 40 men had been arrested and tried, they would have been condemned and shot, and yet they were innocent of the crime of desertion.

Jackson, with his stern, rigid sense of duty, felt differently and would not condone any violation of rules.

General Lee sanctioned the shooting of three men convicted of desertion, in the winter of 1862–63, but never afterward.

He knew that in an army, composed as ours was, of true men, it would be a cruel sacrifice of lives—a two edged sword which would, while striking at a crime, wound our cause in a vital point.

The feelings of the Army were against it. Almost the universal sentiment of the South was opposed to such rigorous construction of martial law.

In very truth, we know that the Southern Armies were composed of men, such as filled the ranks of *no others* since the days of Cæsar, and he—that greatest of all generals and of all men, did not punish soldiers even when guilty of *mutinous revolt*. He only told them to "go home! that they should not serve in Cæsar's Army." That was to them the bitterest condemnation and they sought forgiveness on bended knees.

Suppose for one moment that General Lee had called before him a brigade or a regiment from which men had deserted and said to them "some of your men have tarnished the good name of this Army by deserting its ranks and our cause, go home, if you will; but if you stay your colors shall be taken from you." Does not every one of us know that that condemned Brigade would, in the very next battle, have sought death in the foremost ranks to win back the favor of a beloved chief.

## MARYLAND MEN.

I must here say a word or two of the Maryland men. General S. Cooper, Adjutant General of our Government, told me in Richmond, that over 21,000 Marylanders had entered the Southern Armies. Very unfortunately I think for the good name of our State, and for the success of the cause espoused, these soldiers were never organized into Brigades or Divisions. There were enough to make a corps, and what a corps it would have been; what deeds performed!

General Lee often told me that he had much at heart, the separate organization of the Marylanders. "They are, he said, unrivalled soldiers and if brought together we may get many other Marylanders to join us."

In a letter of May 1865, when I applied after sickness, to join him, he wrote: "I have something better for you. I wish you to take command of the Shenandoah Valley—your headquarters at Staunton. You will have all the Maryland troops, which I hope you will be able to organize and build up into something respectable. You can give general supervision of operations there, and form the left wing of the Army. Let me know your decision and I will issue the necessary orders."

Before I was well enough to reach Staunton, the move into Pennsylvania had begun, and I was swept along with it. And so the collection of Maryland men into Brigades, &c., was never accomplished.

And now my friends, I shall trespass on your patience but a moment longer.

At first we had but one regiment of Marylanders, the gallant 1st. How shall I speak of that? Every one in Lee's and Jackson's Armies admitted the superiority of its martial bearing; its unquestioned bravery and its unequalled discipline. On a march— not hobbling along in broken ranks, but proud and erect in neat fitting uniforms, they "swung on" in platoons of fours, "right shoulder shift," keeping step, "with flag to the breeze." How superb they looked; no "straggling" *there*; on they swept, "dauntless and fearless and free," always welcomed with a cheer as they passed by other troops. They could march better, fight better, make better *biscuits* than any soldiers of the Army.

Oh! if we could have had a Division or Corps of such Soldiers; some of us would have seen more of Maryland and Pennsylvania and stayed there longer I think. I once said to General Lee after the battles around Richmond, when urging the collection of Marylanders together; that with 20,000 such men, he could march to New York. That was "tall bragging." But who can say it might not have been done? The 1st were the "dandies" of the Army; better dressed; better shod; better drilled and in gayer spirits than any in the whole Army, and never *one* deserter.

Who that has stood on some battlefield of the war—made memorable by heroic deeds and dauntless bravery—that was not impressed with deep solemnity in gazing over its features? I have done so, but one year after the war was over, and surveyed with overpowering emotions the plain where

> Bright sword and gleaming bayonet flashed
> In the light of mid-day where serried hosts
> Were shivered; and the grass—green from the soil
> Of carnage; then waved above the crushed
> And mouldering skeleton—where plats of broken soil
> Still *seamed* the plain—showing where "unnamed"
> Graves entombed the fallen dead "names unknown
> To all, but heroes still."

And as my eye fell on these humble hillocks, and my steps profaned not their hallowed earth; I stood with uncovered head and bowed in homage to the heroes who had passed to silence and patriotic dust. And as the glance fell on the undulating surface of that field—its bordering woods; its fences and tangled undergrowth; what sight did memory picture *most* vividly in the conflict that raged there? Was it that noble chieftain, who so much won our love and admiration? Seated calmly, with majestic grandeur, on the old grey horse, and who only loved better the cause he served than the lives of his "boys in gray." The lifting of whose arm made a nation tremble, and whose presence was ever, the inspiration of victory—No! it was not him.

Was it the boom of the great guns on yonder hill—sending and receiving death at every roar—and covering the field with that sulphureous canopy—the battle shroud of those who die! No! it was not the cannon's roar, nor the wild shriek of shot and shell. Then what was it! I'll tell you my comrades.

It was that *long* line of *dusky* forms and flashing bayonets which moves with silent, steady tread across you open field and towards yonder woods,—from which the enemy has, for one hour, sent sheets of leaden hail and from which a fiercer tempest is poured, as those intrepid men advance. The plain is dotted behind them thick with fallen forms. The line grows ragged under this relentless deluge of death—Flags go down; but float again; Still on they go; on; on; on! The wood is near, we hold our breath, and then, above the mad roar of the conflict, there swells upon the air that "Rebel cheer" before which no hostile forces ever stood— and the day is won.

Yes; my comrades; another victory—victory after victory; why—my friends, we were *gorged* with victories, and we begun to loathe them. They were too dearly paid for, by the blood of our brave men, (not the hirelings of foreign lands) and the tears wrung from broken hearts in far-off southern homes.

## VICTORY.

It is said that a victory is sadder even than a defeat. In the latter, we do not realize at once our loss. In the former, we are face to face with the ghastly wounds of the fallen, hear the heart-rending moans of the wounded, and we must perform the saddest of all

sad duties, the task of hunting for and interring our dead comrades.
Then the triumphant cheer is changed to subdued tones, as the
dead are thrown into hastily made graves. There they repose;
no *name*, nor *stone* to mark the spot. Yes; they will march no
more—hunger no more—fight no more—but sleep undisturbed
until the "Great Reveille" shall wake them to a better life; where
wars are not, where no tears are shed nor weariness is known.
Yes; there they slumber; far away from their homes of sunny
childhood. The wild flowers of summer are all that deck these
humble mounds.

> "Which tell of hearts that are waiting in vain
> For those who shall never come home again;
> Of the widow's moan and the orphan's cry
> And the mother's speechless agony."

Ah! no: humble, enduring; patriotic; brave; unselfish;
glorious! "Johnny Reb," you will never be forgotten; you need
no sculptured stone, nor classic epitaph to tell of your deeds.

They will be sung in verse and told in story.

> "When marble wears away,
> And monuments are dust."

But I have detained you too long with this feeble tribute to the
valor and prowess of the Southern infantry and will close by words
from the verse of our sweetest Southern Poet

> "Firm as the firmest where duty led
> He hurried without a falter;
> Bold as the boldest he fought and bled
> And the day was won—but the field was red,
> And the blood of his fresh young heart was shed
> For his country's hallowed altar.
> But their memories e'er shall remain, to us
> Their names—bright names without stain, for us;
> The glory they won shall not wane, for us;
> In legend and lay, our heroes in gray
> Shall forever live over again for us."

# "OUR CAVALRY."

First in the front, last in the rear. The Artillery rested sometimes; the Infantry rarely; the Cavalry never.

RESPONDED TO BY

## LT. COL. CLEMENT SULIVANE,

A. A. G. CUSTIS LEE'S DIVISION, A. N. VA.

There is some indefiniteness about this sentiment which I am called on to respond to, that tends to further embarrass the well known modesty of a cavalry-man. "Always" first in the front and last in the rear." Front of what and rear of what? If it be intended to insinuate that they are always first to sit down at a well spread table, "with concomitants accordin'," and the last to leave it, in allusion to the well known slur of the other corps of the service on the Confederate cavalry, that they were always first in the front to attack the turnip patches and such like other objects of a soldier's love, gracefully retired to the rear at the first sound of heavy guns, and there pertinaciously remained to supply themselves with the *debris* of battle before expeditiously following the infantry and artillery in advance or retreat, then fellow soldiers, I repel the same with indignation.

But the second sub-division of this sentiment seems to forbid the idea of any such intention. "The Artillery sometimes rested, the Infantry rarely, the Cavalry never." Being in the past tense it cannot refer to the present, and can mean but one thing, viz : that the Artillery *sometimes* rested from marching and fighting, the Infantry *rarely*, and the Cavalry *never*. And taking the two together, especially in view of this so happy an occasion that brings so many of us old soldiers together once more, I can but conclude that it is designed as a compliment, and in reply to it on part of my cavalry comrades, will say that we are as happy to meet our old comrades of the Infantry and Artillery on this festive occasion, as (and many a time it has been) we were in the stern days of yore, after weary hours of "holding the situation," to see the long lines of bayonets of the one wheeling into line behind us, and the other unlimbering their cannon in hot haste on the adjacent hill tops. Then indeed "there was music in the air."

But the fact is, Mr. President, it was my fate to serve in all three wings of that famous army, that even in defeat, has added fresh glory to the annals of war, and I think I can speak impartially. Being not much more than an infant, naturally I first served in the Infantry and graduated in that renowned corps under then Capt. (since Colonel) J. Lyle Clark, here present, ably assisted in his tutelage by Lieut. Steuart Symington, seated at my side, who was the "pretty lad" of our company—and I believe the ladies maintain it to this day. Certainly it is not I who will say them nay. Then, like my friend, Col. Jack Wharton, of celebrated memory, being of a somewhat adventurous turn in those days of youth, glory and hope, and having always heard that "if you want to catch h–ll just jine the cavalry," I attached myself to that celebrated corps and had full opportunity for a year and a half to experience the full benefit of the situation. And then I went back to my first love, there to remain until the last guns *but* those of Appomattox resounded over desolated but ever glorious Virginia. I refer of course to "Sailor's Creek." My experience with my friends, the Artillerists, so handsomely represented here to-night by Lieut. Col. McIntosh, was indeed but brief, being in point of fact confined to the volunteer service of a single day, when I became entangled and somewhat mashed up in one of their rascally caissons on that day of blood when, in one broad wave of fiery valor, Infantry, Artillery and Cavalry rolled over the ramparts of Corinth, where (inextricably intermingled) the red, the yellow, and the blue ensigns of the service fell together, and

"Even as they fell in files they lay.
Like the mower's grass at the close of day
When his work is done on the levelled plain,
Such was the fall of the foremost slain."

and cavalry, infantry, and artillery were all alike, the "first in the front and the last in the rear" at the storming of Corinth.

Mr. President, I served during our memorable and disastrous civil struggle from the East to the West and back again to the East, and wherever I went, in *every* branch of the service, I met with Marylanders. And why is it, I will ask, why is it that every Marylander thrills at the name of Maryland? It is because he feels a just pride in his State and of the people of whom he is a unit. It is because he glories in the valor of her sons in the times of war, their enterprise and law-abiding disposition in the days of peace. Because from the commencement of the national history to the present hour—all over the globe—from the icy wastes of Canada far away to the South where the bright green terraces and ever flowering gardens of Mexico, bloom forever beneath the sky of the tropics. On the trackless ocean, where the very war of the elements has been drowned in the thunder of American cannon,

*Wherever* the American flag is flung to the breeze, *there* have throbbed, and still throb, Maryland hearts beneath the uniform of their country. Wherever America has waged war, by land or sea, in protection of the rights, the dignity, and the interests of her people, the children of Maryland have crowded "foremost in the front" and fallen in heaps beneath the banner of the Republic. And as for the rear! who was it that in our last and greatest war got so "full of fight," that seven months after our own Generals told the ragged remnants of us to quit fighting and go home and be as good citizens as we had been soldiers, and that was all they wished of us, and we *never* quit until then—our distinguished guest, the famous Lieutenant General of the army of North Virginia, the most honored as the most renowned of *living* Virginians, exclaims "not by *my* orders"—and I yield to the accuracy of his statement—but it was by order of him who under God commanded us all, Robert E. Lee. I ask you, who was it that aroused the echoes of the deep blue Pacific with Confederate cannon? It was the Captain of the Shenandoah, and he was a Marylander, and his name was Waddell, and he sits by my side. And *his* guns were the re-echoing of echoes that were sounding over the stormy Atlantic, and *they* were those of a Marylander and his name was Semmes. I tell you, gentlemen, that practically Marylanders began that war; the first blood was shed in your own streets of Baltimore, and they certainly ended it. That is to say, and to be entirely accurate, it was a Maryland gun that was fired on the Shenandoah by a South Carolinian whose name was Grimble, a compatriot and friend of the famous Carolinian whom all Maryland delights to honor, the last commander of the cavalry of the army of North Virginia— another distinguished guest who graces us with his presence on this occasion, I can but refer to Lieut. General Wade Hampton of South Carolina. The blood of the sons of Maryland crimsoned the snows of Quebec in the early dawn of the revolution. It was poured out as free as a gushing torrent on the melancholy plains of disastrous Camden, where a Maryland brigade perished well nigh to a man in protecting the retreat of their defeated comrades. And tardy justice is now about to be done, mainly through the instrumentality of the distinguished soldier who presides over this Association, to that renowned foreign soldier who there led our ancestors to battle. Maryland blood reddened the fortifications of Monterey, stained the hoary ramparts of Chapultepec, and rained a ghastly dew on the hill slopes of Gettysburg.

Mr. President, it is not the Confederate survivors of the late desperate struggle between the States who are ashamed of their sleeping comrades, or of the cause in which they fell. Theirs were acts not to be excused but applauded—not to be pardoned but admired. And it is not in this company that I will condescend to vindicate deeds that history will teach the remotest posterity to revere, and which are calculated to enkindle in the hearts of unborn millions the holy enthusiasm of freedom. *We* have already placed their names—side by side with the heroes of the revolution, of the war of 1812, and of Mexico, and garlanded with the *immortelles* that belong to the fallen brave, in that niche in the Temple of Fame where they will be preserved sacred and inviolate through all the ages. At least, while liberty remains a name upon earth and self-sacrificing patriotism and unflinching courage are honored among men. We revere their memory, we justify the cause in which they have fallen, and I trust I may hope and say in conclusion, Gentlemen of Maryland, that should any proper occasion arise, we of this generation may be found equal to the task of emulating their example.

# "OUR ARTILLERY."

Though occasionally their room was better than their company, by reason of the marked attention which they attracted from the enemy, as a rule they were very welcome—except to the people opposite.

RESPONDED TO BY

COL. DAVID G. McINTOSH,

McINTOSH'S BATTALION ARTILLERY, A. N. VA.

Mr. President and Fellow Comrades:

It is such a very long while since I have had anything to do with trailing a gun, or handling a battery; I am afraid, in endeavoring to respond to this toast to the "Artillery," I shall find I have almost forgotten how to "unlimber" and come into "action front."

I congratulate myself however, that on this occasion, I need be in no hurry to get the range of an enemy; that there is no botheration about ascertaining the true difference between the "line of sight" and the "line of fire;" that I have no "Hausses" to look through, and no "Horses" to look after; and that I can quietly throw a harmless shell, only taking care that my fuse be not cut too long.

I am reminded by the terms in which you have been pleased to convey this toast, that there were times, when our room was preferred to our company, and our brothers of the Cavalry and the Infantry did'nt care to have the Artillery as near neighbors, by reason of the attention bestowed upon them by the other side.

I cannot undertake to speak for those branches of the service, but speaking for the Artillery, I think I am safe in saying that such a feeling was never reciprocated on their side. They may have been a little exclusive about the matter of camps; and I think I have heard of their anxiety to get as far away to themselves as possible; because perhaps of an impression which generally prevailed, that Hardee's tactics didn't lay sufficient stress on the distinction between *meum* and *tuum*.

But whenever there was a fight on hand, we were as social as possible; we always loved company then; and we were ready to embrace our Infantry Brothers, and be embraced by them even to two or three lines deep. I think about the lonesomest feeling in the world, certainly the lonesomest to an Artilleryman, is to be expecting a charge every moment and not be able to see any support around.

One of the lonesomest experiences of that sort which came to my knowledge, happened during that campaign about which we have been so eloquently entertained by the distinguished speaker of the evening.

28

While the famished men and horses were luxuriating on the stores captured at Manassas Junction, a battery was ordered to take position upon the crest of a hill some distance to the south to meet an apprehended attack from the direction of Bristow Station. Which they proceeded to do *without their stores.*

The afternoon saw all the troops in the neighborhood move off to the north, and night came on, but no word to the Battery. The hours grew longer as the darkness increased, and an occasional scout sent out reported nothing behind but the smoking ruins at the Junction, and nothing in front but the ominous rumbling of moving trains. Long after midnight a squad of passing cavalry gave the soothing intelligence that they brought up the rear guard of the army, and that the enemy wasn't far off. You've heard of the boy that stood on the burning deck ; but there wasn't any Casabianca in that Battery on that night. Those boys didn't want to be burned up or gobbled up ; they concluded it was too utterly lonesome, and day-light next morning found them at Centreville behind as many lines of Infantry as they could find.

But Mr. President, in responding to a sentiment, offered as this is, to a branch of the service representing so many brave and distinguished men, I am afraid I should appear wanting in proper respect, if I allowed my remarks to be made altogether in the spirit of levity.

It has its painful reminders, but it has also much that none of us would be willing to blot out or extinguish.

It is not easy to speak of the past just as one feels, or as one would like.

There is something in the discipline and the danger and privations of a soldier's life, which always make its retrospect the tenderest spot in his life. He nurses its memory with tender solicitude, and no matter how rich or how poor, he esteems it among the costliest of his earthly possessions.

When these of us therefore who know something of what that experience means, meet together in these annual reunions, the world outside may well excuse us if we pause for a moment again to look each other in the face, and briefly renew the associations begotten in the past. There isn't a true soldier to-day, on either side who would exchange his army experience for any period of his life of equal duration.

I take it therefore there is no arrogance or conceit, no,—nor disloyalty either—in saying I am proud of my association with the Artillery of the Army of Northern Virginia.

None of us can be insensible to the impressions which the last twenty years have made : we are all of us to some extent moulded by events.

Perhaps few, if any of those who fought the stoutest, would now wish to change the final issue of the struggle. The thing which most concerns us, and that which must assuredly be accorded to us by History, is that in doing what we did, we did under a solemn sense of duty. It was the sense of duty and the supreme conviction that right was on our side, which made us the soldiers that we were.

It would be envidious, Mr. President, and perhaps in bad taste for me to allude specially on this occasion to the part which the Artillery bore in our memorable struggle.

For myself, I have always concluded that to the Infantry man in the ranks, belongs the first place of Honor. And I remember that when I was accustomed to see those little squads mustered at nightfall from their respective regiments and detailed to creep out to the trenches on the picket line, there to lie for twenty four hours in the mud and ice, between the lines of opposing forces only a few hundred yards apart. I always felt like lifting my hat to them as par excellence, the heroes of our army.

But while the Artillery had little opportunity for the display of dash, and were denied the thrill of that exulting joy which runs along the line of a victorious charge ; and while their chief merit lay in the exercise of passive obedience and dogged resistance, there was now and then an exhibition of their daring temper as well as their stubborn courage.

I trust you will pardon my recalling an instance. I accompanied Dement's Maryland Battery when a division of our Army attacked the left flank of the enemy, near the Weldon railroad, in front of Petersburg. The movement was quick and rapid, but the battery moving thro' an open space on the edge of the wood, kept abreast of our front line of battle, firing as it advanced, and when the battle was over, and while we were gathering in the captured guns and prisoners, a section of the battery commanded by the gallant soldier who now sits near me, Lieutenant Hill, taking out their horses ran their guns by hand in front of our pickets, and within 200 yards of the enemy's works, firing several rounds of cannister in the very face of the enemy and getting off without a scratch.

Amid all the glorious achievements of our army in every branch, there isn't a more brilliant episode than the defense of Fort Gregg, garrisoned by the Chesapeake Artillery and the "Sups" from the battalion, armed with muskets, and nicknamed "Walker's mules." The proper history of that defence has yet to be written. I saw column after column of heavy black masses of troops broken and shattered by the fire from the guns in the works, and when after repeated efforts the enemy succeeded in crossing the moat and scaling the rampart, I could see the flash of the guns, with the enemy at their muzzles, and the gunners bayoneted at their posts.

I cannot, Mr. President, in the short space of time within which I am cautioned to burn my fuse, venture to allude to the personnel of the Artillery. But I must be permitted to offer a single word by way of tribute to that good man and distinguished soldier, who was the Chief of Artillery of the Army of Northern Virginia and whose death has been recorded since our last meeting.

He first saw service as Captain of a battery with Colonel, afterwards General Stonewall Jackson ; was conspicuous with his smooth brass guns at the first Manassas, and was made Chief of Artillery first under Gen'l Johnson, and then under Gen'l Lee. It was in the last capacity that I knew him.

The organization of the Artillery was such that it could never be handled as a whole, and there was little opportunity for the display of ability on the part of a Chief, except in the general efficiency of that arm of the service. In this respect, General Pendleton displayed the most excellent judgment, and his directions and suggestions on the field were always marked by great prudence and sagacity. One had only to see and speak with him a moment, to discover that he was not only the educated, but the christian soldier. He often received honorable mention in the official reports of the Campaign, and he possessed, I believe, the entire confidence of that great leader, whom we all trusted and delighted to follow. His great and beloved commander went before him, and now, he too has crossed over that river, upon the banks of which, we still pitch our tents, and has passed to the other shore.

If we carry with us aught of the human into that spirit-land, we may well believe, he rejoices in communion with those illustrious shadows, by whom on earth he was loved and esteemed.

In conclusion, let me say, Mr. President, that if as a rule, we were welcome to our side, we did our level best to make ourselves unwelcome to the other side. They beat us in the amount of ammunition burned; and until we had captured sufficient to make up a fair average, they excelled us in the character of our ordnance; but when it came to the point of markmanship and execution, I believe our gunners always held their own.

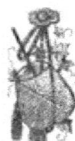

# "OUR NAVY"

Ready for service wherever duty called; in the batteries at
Acquia Creek, or in the breast-works at Petersburg;
from Hampton Roads to Mobile Bay, in the hour of
disaster not less than in the day of victory;
they added lustre to the cause they loved;
they made all seas acquainted with
our flag; they bore it farthest and
they furled it last.

RESPONDED TO BY

## CAPT. JAMES J. WADDELL,

C. S. S. S. SHENANDOAH.

L. of C.

MR. PRESIDENT AND GENTLEMEN:

Your honorable committee have paid me the distinguished compliment, by request, to respond to that sentiment, "Our Navy." To me, as with all of us, it is an interesting feature to this evening's entertainment. A sailor, with his opportunities, hesitates to fulfill the duty he has undertaken to perform, in addressing an audience cultured in all those branches of educational refinement which develop and embellish the intellectual attributes of man. Mr. President, the theme of this response, like the flag it bore, though dead, yet will live; and I shall talk about these things which occupied the thoughts of my boyhood, grew with my growth into manhood, and have ever fascinated my understanding.

The personnel of the "Navy of the Confederate States" has written its history in human gore. And I need here not descant on the odds it met, the places where conflicts and results occurred, but like its heroism, so has it become history; that it gave to the Naval powers of the World, the armour plated fighting ships. All the powers of Europe, if they would do the honest thing, would pay Captain Brooke a royalty, to say nothing of the Government under whose flag we must feel privileged to live, and be content. The illustrious names of "Buchanan" and of "Semmes" in themselves constitute a Navy. Without such spirits, iron and wooden ships of war mean nothing; it is the inspiration of the God-like soul which throws light into such material, and those names go down to coming generations, a people's pride, a people's glory, a people's history. And Mr. President, *their memories leave emulation panting behind.* The cruising vessels of the Confederate States were intended to operate against the enemy's commerce, they were few, slightly built and swift, and those vessels took absolute possession of the waters of the world, *driving* without opposition the enemy's mercantile marine from the ocean—that were so fortunate as to escape capture—into port and *even there*, the "Gallant Read" chased and captured them.

As champions of a cause which commended itself, even to those whose political instincts it offended, tribute has been offered to their patriotism and to their country's chivalry. No greater compliment could be paid them than the enemy's running abuse for twenty years. It has been charged them that they were content with burning merchantmen and destroying the commerce of the enemy, and as they did only what every belligerent power is most ambitious of doing to its opponent, the charge is a *testimony to their activity and skill*. They may well be excused for using a weapon that their enemy had furnished them; if *privateering — as they still will have it — was the vice of the Confederates*, then the "Federals" are responsible for having sanctioned it; if it was the one engine of war, which harrassed them most, then they reaped the penalty of having fabricated it. It is well-known that when Europe conspired to put down the system, America refused to divest warfare of one of its most cruel accessions. Sum up the offenses against civilization, of which both sides were guilty, and then see which is the greater criminal. Have the people, who speak of the Captains of those cruisers as "Pirates," ever heard of the *theft* of the "Florida?" The Federal Government distinguished itself formerly in this class of transactions, but did never suppress the outrages in the Brazillian waters, on the 4th of October, 1864. Did it ever give a more conspicuous exhibition of the code of law and honor which ruled it, and which its apologists affected to dispise in their opponents? We all recollect the tale of treachery. The "Florida" arrived at Bahia San Salvador, on the 4th of October, 1864, she put in for a supply of stores and coal and to repair her machinery. Soon after she anchored, a boat came alongside and asked her name. The Confederate gave his reply in all honesty. A person in the boat responded, "this boat is from Her Britannic Majesty's Steamer Curlew." *The thing was untrue*, for no British man-of-war was in port at that time. The "Florida" was discovered, and in a few hours, in the dead of night, so history goes, her crew was butchered and the vessel towed out of port and taken to Hampton Roads, where, we all know how and by whom, she was destroyed—that destruction was made to avoid an honest restitution. The commander of the "Washusetts" was made a commodore for his seizure of the "Florida" in neutral waters. I do not think it would have occurred in a British or a French port. It has been said if the Confederate Government had bought more cruisers and let the building of costly fighting ships alone, a different result may have been reached; that I think questionable. To build fighting ships abroad was an easy task, but to get them to sea and man them was a difficult one. Sailors are like other men, they do not relish the thought of having their brains knocked out in another man's fight. We depended on foreign sailors, and they felt no interest in our war; a thirst for gain allured a few to enlist in our Ocean service, and prize money was the inducement. A sailor's devotion while serving in a ship grows, and at mention of her name his heart warms, and he is ever ready to defend her honor, hence the restless impatience of the "Alabama's" crew to engage the "Kearsarge."

What else, except the sailor's belief, in the life of ships, makes the parallel between ship's lives and men's life, so pleasant and constant a fable? as on land, so on sea, you have them of all sorts. There is the national ship, proud, stately, warlike. There is the great merchantman, rich, solid, busy. There is the fat, bustling trader, toiling up and down the coast with coals or cattle or produce. There are the graceful, lively, gaily dressed pleasure craft, yachts and dispatch boats, *the ladies of the sea.* There are the industrious, disregarded "smacks" and "pungies" working hard for every inch of luck they get and taking the weather pretty much as it comes, which nobody counts, and nobody cares for. And the reason why a ship's fate affects you so much, is always the sailor's reason. When we see a great vessel rolling lonely at sea, her mast gone, her gear loose and adrift, and sheets of foaming sea pouring in and out of her helpless sides; who wants the fable explained? Many such a craft, once proud and capable, wallows among the screaming sea birds of destiny, upon the waters of life.

Practical and imaginative people may say: what difference does it make to the ship? but no sailor will listen to that. Loquacious theorists have declared, that naval supremacy is due to a pronoun, we call the ship *"the"* and other tongues call a ship *"it."* "She" implies that the ship *"carries us"* and in some manner, alive, as a sailor in his heart privately believes—or why does he talk about her foot, her waist, her head, her dimity, as the graceful thing floats on the surface of the ocean? There is life in the craft, from the time she leaves the "ways" into the tide, to the hour when her timbers are laid on the sand or rocks, or the saddest of all, in the ship breaker's yard. The most of the iron plated vessel is, that the black, ugly armour has no such vitality, and cannot be christened with the pretty old fashioned names which helped the sailor's superstition out. We cannot answer for such hideous monsters, they are created out of dull mineral, which came from the bowels of the earth, and should they not all come to grief like the "Monitor?" The "Blacksmith," will some day have to turn them into, *pots and pans, iron railings and boilers*, but Mr. President, the timber of the wooden ship grew in the sunlight, it waved in the forest and heard the winds sing, before bending to the breeze under topsails.

www.ingramcontent.com/pod-product-compliance
Lightning Source LLC
Chambersburg PA
CBHW032244080426
42735CB00008B/1003